Shine On

A STORY BIBLE

Presented to

_____

FROM _____

ON _____

Shine On
A STORY BIBLE

SHiNE
Living in God's Light

MennoMedia
Harrisonburg, Virginia
Kitchener, Ontario

Brethren Press
Elgin, Illinois

Library of Congress Cataloging-in-Publication Data
Shine on : a story Bible.
    pages cm
 ISBN 978-0-8361-9856-0 (hardcover : alk. paper) 1. Bible stories, English.
 BS551.3.S543 2014
 220.95'05--dc23

                              2013038445

SHINE ON: A STORY BIBLE
Copyright © 2014 by MennoMedia, Harrisonburg, Virginia 22802 and Brethren Press, Elgin, Illinois 60120.
Released simultaneously in Canada by MennoMedia, Kitchener, Ontario N2G 3R1. All rights reserved.
Library of Congress Control Number: 2013038445
International Standard Book Number: 978-0-8361-9856-0
Printed in Canada.
Editors: Rebecca Seiling, Anna M. Speicher, and Rose Mary Stutzman
Consulting editor: Carrie Martens
Art direction, cover, and book design: Merrill R. Miller
Cover art: Kate Cosgrove

Unless otherwise noted, Scripture text is quoted, with permission, from the New Revised Standard Version, © 1989, Division of Christian Education of the National Council of Churches of Christ in the United States of America.

To order or request information, visit ShineCurriculum.com.

18 17 16 15 14   10 9 8 7 6 5 4 3

Introduction

God's light: breaking through in creation, coming into the world through Jesus, and shining today in our lives. Jesus said, "You are the light of the world." This thread of light, woven through the Bible, is now passed on to you through engaging stories and colorful images demonstrating the rich witness of the people of God.

The stories in *Shine On: A Story Bible* include a whole cast of characters, some wily, some wise. All are wrestling to know God and give us a glimpse of God's desire for the world.

For Christians, the Bible is a rare and precious treasure, an inspiration and guide for our lives. It is a place where we come to listen to God.

People passed on these stories for many generations, sitting near a fire or in a town square or around a meal at home. Through spoken words, they preserved their memories about how God was acting among them. Long ago, scribes wrote the words onto scrolls. Centuries later, the scrolls were made into a library of books from Genesis to Revelation, called the Bible. This tradition of sharing these stories now rests with you and your community of faith.

Shine On is not meant to be only for children. It is our hope that this collection will be shared, discussed, and read together as a family and community of faith. *Shine On* highlights the wealth of biblical material (stories, poetry, songs, laws, instructions, history) and includes a range of selections from both Old and New Testaments. A variety of artists created the beautiful illustrations. Each story is accompanied with questions, prayers, or activities that encourage spiritual practices and invite readers to wonder and reflect, connect the story to their own lives, and further explore the story's meaning.

These stories present anew the exciting, curious, wonderful account of God at work in the world with flawed, genuine people. They inspire children and adults to discuss, question, and act in response to the biblical message.

Do you want to shine a light in your community, in your world? Go ahead—open this book. Read a story together and listen carefully. What do you hear? How is it moving you to follow God? If we allow them, these stories can transform us into the people God is calling us to be. Together, we can encourage God's light to shine on.

—*Rebecca Seiling and Rose Mary Stutzman*

Contents

New Testament

Let there be light!

Genesis 1:1–5; Psalm 119:105, 130; Isaiah 9:2; Matthew 5:14–16; John 1:1–9

Connect
God's light is with us in good times and bad. Light a candle in a dark room. Choose your favorite scripture from this story and read it aloud. Be a light in the world around you!

Light is mentioned again and again in the Bible. God's light fills the empty darkness from the beginning of time. God's light guides our path through life. The light shines in the darkness and the darkness cannot overcome the light.

In the beginning, darkness covered the face of the deep and God said, "Let there be light!" And there was light—bright, good light. God separated the light from the darkness and called the light "day" and the darkness "night."

A song from the Bible in the book of Psalms says, "Your word is a lamp to my feet and a light to my path. The unfolding of your words gives light."

In difficult times the prophet Isaiah brought this message to the Israelites, "The people who walked in darkness have seen a great light; those who lived in a land of deep darkness—on them light has shined." God's message brought hope and courage.

Later, John the Baptist told people that Jesus was coming. The true light, which gives light to everyone, was coming into the world. Jesus showed God's love to all. Jesus is the true light.

Jesus sat on a mountainside and taught his followers. "You are the light of the world!" Jesus said. "A city on a hill cannot be hidden. Nobody lights a lamp and puts it under a bushel basket. It is put on a lampstand, where it can give light to everyone in the whole house. In the same way, let your light shine before others. They will see your good works and give thanks to God."

The light shines in the darkness and the darkness cannot put it out.

Wonder: I wonder why light is so important in the Bible.

Explore

Today we can make light using various technologies: solar-powered light, electrical light, fire, LED lights, fluorescent lights, and many more. What types of lights can you find in your home?

God creates the world

Genesis 1:1–2:3

Connect

You are created in God's image! Look around and notice the goodness of creation. How can we care for creation?

In the beginning there was only darkness.

Wind swept over the waters, and God said, "Let there be light!" and there was light. God called the light "day" and the darkness "night." And there was evening and there was morning, the first day.

God said, "Let there be a dome that separates the waters above from the waters below." God made the dome and called it "sky." And there was evening and there was morning, the second day.

God said, "Let the waters under the sky be gathered into one place, and let the dry land appear." God called the dry land "earth" and the waters "seas." Then God said, "Let the earth be filled with plants and trees and fruits and seeds." God saw that it was good. And there was evening and there was morning, the third day.

God said, "Let there be lights in the sky to separate the day from the night." And it was so. God made the sun to shine by day and the moon to shine by night. God saw that it was good. And there was evening and there was morning, the fourth day.

And God said, "Let the waters be filled with fish and living creatures. Let the sky be filled with birds flying above the earth." God saw that it was good. God blessed them saying, "Fill the seas and the sky." And there was evening and there was morning, the fifth day.

And God said, "Let the earth be filled with creatures of every kind." God said, "Let us make humans in our image, who can care for the fish and birds and animals of the earth." God made humans, male and female. God blessed them and said, "Fill the earth and care for the earth and for all living things." God saw that everything was very good. And there was evening and there was morning, the sixth day.

On the seventh day, God rested. God blessed the seventh day and set it apart as a special day of rest.

Wonder: Think about the world being spoken or sung into being. Read one paragraph and picture the broad sweeping changes.

Explore

Scientists estimate that there are thirty million different species of insects on the planet and that some ten quintillion insects are alive at any given time. More species are being discovered each year.

Connect

Plan a garden that you could tend, even if it is just one small pot on your porch. Growing food is a fun project to do as a family. What would you like to grow?

14

Explore
Find the names of four rivers in the garden (Genesis 2:10–14). Do Internet research on each of the river names. Which two rivers can still be found on maps today? What meanings and places are connected with the other two rivers?

God tends a garden in Eden

Genesis 2:4–19

In the day that God made the earth and the heavens—before there were plants; even before it had ever rained—a stream rose and watered the ground.

Then God formed a man from the dust of the ground. God breathed into the man's nostrils and he became alive.

God planted a beautiful garden in Eden. God made every type of tree grow up from the ground. These trees were wonderful and full of delicious fruit. In the middle of the garden grew the tree of life. Beside it was another tree—the tree of the knowledge of good and evil.

A river flowed out of this beautiful, green garden and it became four rivers, flowing around lands with gold and onyx stone.

God took the man and put him in the garden of Eden to care for the land.

God said, "You may eat of every tree in the garden except for the tree of the knowledge of good and evil. If you eat from that tree, you will die."

God formed every living creature. Animals and birds came to the man to be cared for and named.

Wonder: Imagine God breathing life into people and living creatures. Imagine the scene in which the creatures are being named.

Explore

What are the rules in your home that you are expected to follow? Talk with your family about the rules that help you live together with love.

Trouble in the garden

Genesis 3

Adam and Eve lived in the garden of Eden. They walked among the animals and ate tasty foods that grew on green trees. They drank water from clear, clean streams. Each evening they walked joyfully through the trees and talked with God. Each day Adam and Eve thought, "It's a beautiful garden. God made a good world."

Then one day the craftiest of the animals talked to Eve. This talking serpent asked, "Did God say, 'You shall not eat from any tree in the garden?'"

"We may eat of the fruit of the trees in the garden," answered Eve. "But God said, 'You shall not eat of the fruit of the tree that is in the middle of the garden.'"

"Ah," said the serpent, "but when you eat the fruit you will be like God, knowing good and evil."

So both Adam and Eve ate the fruit. When the sun went down, Adam and Eve hid instead of walking in the cool evening breeze.

"Where are you?" asked God.

"We're hiding because we're afraid," whispered Adam and Eve from behind some leaves.

"Have you eaten from the tree in the middle of the garden?" asked God.

"Yes," said Adam. "Eve gave me some and I ate it."

"Yes," said Eve. "The serpent tricked me."

God said that the serpent would now crawl on its belly. Life changed for Adam and Eve too. God made clothes for Adam and Eve and sent them out of the garden. The perfect and peaceful garden was a thing of the past. They were often lonely, sad, or frightened. Adam and Eve had to work hard to grow food. They pulled thorns, thistles, and weeds from the ground and planted seeds.

Although much had changed in their lives, Adam and Eve could still choose to trust God. God had come looking for them. God had provided clothes for them. They could learn to live and care in God's good world.

Wonder: I wonder what it was like to talk to God.

Jealousy between brothers

Genesis 4:1–16

Connect
What can you do when you feel jealous or angry? Make a poster for your refrigerator that lists some ideas.

Adam and Eve had two sons, Cain and Abel. Cain was a farmer, growing grains and vegetables. Abel was a shepherd, caring for a flock of sheep.

One day, each of the brothers brought an offering to God. Cain brought grain from his fields. Abel brought some of the firstborn lambs in his flock.

God accepted Abel's offering but did not accept Cain's. Cain's face fell. God asked Cain, "Why are you so angry? If you handle yourself well, you will be accepted. Your feelings want to control you," God warned Cain, "but you can master them."

But Cain continued to feed his anger. He found Abel and said, "Come into the field with me." When they were there, Cain's anger and jealousy overwhelmed him and he killed his brother.

God spoke to Cain again, saying, "Where is your brother Abel?"

"I don't know," Cain lied. "Am I my brother's keeper?"

"What have you done, Cain?" God asked. Cain did not answer.

God said, "Listen! Abel's blood is crying out to me from the ground. Now, Cain, you will be cursed from the ground. You will not be able to till the land and grow food to feed yourself. You will be a fugitive and a wanderer."

Cain cried out to God, "This punishment is more than I can bear. Today you have driven me away from the soil, and I will be hidden from your face. I will be a fugitive and a wanderer on the earth, and anyone who meets me may kill me."

"No!" God told Cain. "Anyone who tries to kill you will suffer greatly." Then God put a mark on Cain, so that no one would kill him. Cain went away to live the rest of his life separated from his family and his land. He settled in the land of Nod, east of Eden.

Wonder: How could Cain have handled his anger differently?

Noah and God's promises

Genesis 6:5–9:17

Connect

In Genesis 9:13, God sets a bow in the clouds. This can be understood to mean that God is declaring peace by setting down a weapon. When you see a rainbow, you can pray: *Thank you, God, for your promise of peace.*

People filled the earth with wars and suffering. Kindness and love almost disappeared. God grieved over the fighting and evil in the world.

In that world filled with violence, Noah chose God's ways. Noah found favor with God.

God told Noah, "A flood will destroy all you know. Build an ark of cypress wood and cover it with pitch inside and out so that it is watertight. Make rooms in the ark. Bring a male and female of every living creature—birds, creeping things, wild animals, and tame animals. Store food on the ark for all the animals."

So Noah and his family gathered food. The animals entered the ark two by two. Noah and his wife, their sons and their son's wives, all went into the ark to escape the coming flood.

It rained for forty days and forty nights. The waters rose until even the mountains were covered. The boat floated like a lonely island on the floodwaters.

The waters finally went down enough for the boat to rest on a mountaintop. Noah sent out a raven to fly to and fro over the earth. Then, Noah sent out a dove but it came right back to him. A week later, Noah sent the dove out again. This time the dove returned with an olive branch in its beak.

Noah waited another week, then sent the dove again. This time the dove did not return. Noah opened up the ark. The animals went out with their families. Noah and his family came out too. They built an altar and worshiped God.

God said to Noah and his family, "I have set my bow in the clouds. This is the sign of the promise that I am making to you and all the creatures on earth. Never again shall there be a flood to destroy the earth. As long as the earth endures, seedtime and harvest, cold and heat, summer and winter, day and night, shall not cease."

Wonder: I wonder if it was hard for Noah to follow God's ways when others didn't.

Explore

Our choices can lead to destruction of animals, land, and oceans. Read about endangered species, both plant and animal. How can we help to protect our diverse creatures, plants, water, and habitats?

The Tower of Babel

Genesis 11:1–9

Connect
Read the story of Pentecost on page 280 to hear how people of many language groups could understand each other. How can you work together with others even if we don't speak the same language?

Everyone in the whole world spoke the same language. The people said to each other, "Come, let's make some bricks." Together, they made many, many bricks.

Then they said, "Come, let's build a city. Let's make a huge tower that reaches up to heaven. We'll be famous! If we don't do this, we'll be scattered around the whole world."

So the people began to build.

God saw the city and the tower that the people were building. God said, "This is one group of people, and they all speak the same language. This is only the beginning of what they will do. Nothing that they can imagine will be impossible for them! Come, let's go down and confuse their speaking so that they cannot understand each other."

So God gave the people different languages, and they became confused. Neighbors couldn't understand each other. The builders were frustrated; they couldn't communicate well enough to get anything done.

They stopped building the city. The place was named Babel, because there God confused the language of the whole world and from there God scattered people far and wide.

Wonder: I wonder what God wished the people would do with their building skills.

Explore

In Hebrew, the word *babal* means "to confuse." In the ancient world, a *ziggurat* was a temple tower built to reach to the heavens. It had many levels and was often made with sun-baked bricks.

Left: the hanging gardens of Babylon. **Right:** the step pyramid of King Zoser, Saqqara, Egypt.

Connect

When you try new things, how do you feel? Think about a time when you moved to a new place, or made a new friend, or started going to a new school.

Explore
God called Abram and Sarai to go. Talk to your family members about when they have heard God calling them to do something.

Abram, Sarai, and Lot

Genesis 12–13

Abram journeyed from Ur with his father to the land of Haran. Later, God told Abram, "Go from this country to the land that I will show you. I will bless you and make your name great. I will make you into a great nation."

So Abram, Sarai, and Abram's nephew Lot followed God. They moved away from their home country. They moved many times and Abram and Lot always pitched their tents close to each other. Abram had livestock, silver, and gold. Lot had flocks of sheep and herds of cattle. Each year, there were more and more animals. It was hard to find water and enough grass for so many animals.

"We need this grass for our cows and sheep," said Lot's workers.

"This is our grass. Go find your own grass," said Abram's workers.

"Let's not fight over whose cows eat where," said Abram to Lot. "Look to your left. Look to your right. There's plenty of land for us to share. You choose first then I'll go in the other direction."

Lot looked to the left and looked to the right. Lot chose the land close to the Jordan River. The fields were as green as a garden.

Abram and Sarai went the other way, to the land of Canaan. Then God gave Abram a message and promise:

"Raise your eyes.

Look to the north. Look to the south.

Look to the east and west.

I will give you the lands from here to there.

I will give you a large family with whom to share.

You will have as many children as the specks of dust on the earth."

Abram and Sarai settled by the oaks of Mamre near Hebron. They built an altar and worshiped God who had promised to bless them.

Wonder: How do you think Abram and Sarai felt about moving to a new land? Curious? Nervous? Excited?

Connect

Baby Isaac brought much laughter and joy. What child makes you feel happy? How have you been blessed?

Explore

In several Bible stories, people change their names when something important happens. Sometimes this is when they make a promise to God. Look at Genesis 35:10 and Acts 13:9 for other examples of name changes in the Bible.

God's promises to Abraham and Sarah

Genesis 16:1–17:22; 18:1–15; 21:1–7

Abram and Sarai knew that children are a blessing from God. God had promised many children to Abram, but years passed and he and Sarai did not have any children. Sarai decided that Hagar, her slave, would have children for her. So when baby Ishmael was born, he had two mothers. Hagar was his birth mother. Sarai was his other mother.

God said to Hagar, "I will bless Ishmael. He will have many children. His children, grandchildren, and great-great-grandchildren will be a great nation."

When Abram was ninety-nine years old, God appeared to him and gave him a new name. Abram became Abraham, the father of many. God also said that Sarai would now be called Sarah. Again, God promised that Abraham and Sarah would have many children.

At about that time, three visitors came walking by the tents of Abraham and Sarah. Abraham invited them to stay for some bread and meat. The visitors brought a message from God. They said, "Sarah is going to have a baby." Sarah laughed at that idea. She was far too old to have a baby. God asked Abraham, "Why did Sarah laugh? Is anything too difficult for the Lord?"

It came to pass just as the three visitors had said. Sarah gave birth to a son in her old age. Abraham and Sarah named him Isaac, which means laughter.

Sarah said, "God has brought laughter for me; everyone who hears this story will laugh with me." Baby Isaac blessed many people with joy and laughter.

Ishmael and Isaac were signs of God's promise to Abraham and Sarah.

Wonder: Imagine having three messengers bring you good news from God.

God hears Hagar and Ishmael

Genesis 16:1–15; 21:8–21

Connect

Have you ever felt sad and troubled by the way someone has acted toward you? Bring this sadness to God in prayer, breathing in as you say, "God," and breathing out as you say, "be with me."

Sarah thought that she wanted her slave Hagar to have a child for her and Abraham. But when Hagar got pregnant, Sarah was jealous. She treated Hagar so badly that Hagar ran away.

God's angel found Hagar near a spring of water. "Hagar, where did you come from and where are you going?" Hagar said, "I am running away from my mistress, Sarah."

The angel said, "You must return. You will become the mother of a multitude of children." Hagar did return and gave birth to Ishmael.

Then Sarah had her own baby, Isaac. When Isaac was old enough to eat solid foods, Abraham prepared a celebration. On the day of the feast, Sarah saw Ishmael playing with his little brother Isaac.

"Send Hagar and her son away," said Sarah to Abraham. "The son of this slave woman shall not inherit along with my son Isaac."

Abraham loved Ishmael and was very distressed. But God told him to do as Sarah wished.

The next morning, Abraham sent Hagar and Ishmael away with some bread and a skin of water. Hagar and Ishmael wandered around in the dry wilderness of Beersheba. Soon the water was gone and Ishmael became weak with thirst. Hagar found a small bush to shade Ishmael. She walked away from the bush and then she sat down and wept. She cried out, "Do not let me see my child die."

God heard the voice of the boy, and the angel of God called to Hagar. "Do not be afraid, Hagar. Come, hold Ishmael close to you."

Then God opened Hagar's eyes and she saw a well of water. She went and filled her waterskin and gave Ishmael a drink.

God was with Ishmael as he grew up in the wilderness of Paran. Ishmael became an expert hunter with his bow and arrow. When he grew up, Hagar arranged for Ishmael to have a wife from Egypt, her home country.

Wonder: God heard Hagar's cries for help. I wonder who God hears; who God helps.

Explore

Find Ishmael in the shade of the bush. Who are the people in your community who feel rejected and troubled? What could your family or friends do for these people?

30

Connect

How do you follow God's leading? Pray together as a family to ask where God is leading you to serve and help others.

God leads Rebekah

Genesis 24

Abraham was getting old. He wanted his son Isaac to marry a good woman from the land where he had been born. Abraham decided to send his servant to look for a wife for Isaac. He gave the man some helpers and ten camels, and many beautiful gifts of gold and jewelry and rich garments.

They traveled for many days and finally came to Abraham's hometown. The servant stopped by a well of water. He prayed, "God of my master Abraham, please give me success and show your love to Abraham. When I ask for a drink of water, let the girl who serves me also offer to serve the camels. Let this young woman be the one you have chosen to become Isaac's wife."

Before he had finished praying, a girl named Rebekah came out to fill her jar at the well. The servant said, "Please let me sip a little water from your jar." Rebekah answered, "Drink, and I will also get water for your camels."

The servant quietly watched Rebekah, wondering if she was the one God had chosen for Isaac. When the camels finished drinking, he gave Rebekah a gold nose-ring and two gold bracelets. He asked, "Is there room in your family's house for us to spend the night?"

Rebekah answered, "Yes, we have plenty of food and bedding for your camels and a place for you to spend the night." The servant followed Rebekah to her home and her family welcomed him. He told them about his mission from Abraham, and he gave Rebekah and her mother and brother the gifts he had brought. He asked if they were willing for Rebekah to return with him and marry Isaac.

Rebekah said, "Yes, I will go with this man and marry Isaac." Her family blessed her and sent her on her way.

When they arrived, Isaac came walking out of the field to meet them, and the servant told him the story of what he had done. Rebekah married Isaac and Isaac loved her very much.

Wonder: What might it have been like for Rebekah to leave home and marry somebody she had never met?

Isaac and the wells

Genesis 26:12–33

Connect
Talk together about what to do when you have a problem. When is it best to walk away from a problem the way Isaac did?

Isaac, Rebekah, and their children settled in the land of Gerar. God blessed Isaac. His crops grew bountifully and he became rich. He had many animals and servants. Even though the land was dry, Isaac had wells with plenty of water.

Isaac's neighbors became jealous of Isaac and they decided to fill his wells with dirt. King Abimelech was afraid of Isaac because of his wealth and power. He told Isaac, "Move away from us. You have become too powerful."

So Isaac moved away. He took his family and his servants and all of his animals to a different place. Isaac's household dug new wells. But soon the neighboring herders argued with Isaac's herders and said, "This water is ours!"

So Isaac moved from there and dug another well. This time no one quarreled over it; and he called it Rehoboth. He said, "Now God has made room for us, and we will be fruitful in the land."

From there, Isaac and his family traveled to a place called Beersheeba. That night God appeared to Isaac and said, "I am the God of your father, Abraham. Do not be afraid of anything because I am with you. I will bless you and your children."

Isaac built an altar there and worshiped God. His servants started digging a new well.

Then King Abimelech came with two of his men to visit Isaac. Isaac asked them, "Why are you here? Didn't you send me away from you?" They answered, "Now we know that God is with you. We want to make a promise with you never to hurt each other."

Isaac prepared a big feast and they ate together. Early the next morning they made promises to each other and parted in peace.

Wonder: I wonder how the king came to realize that God was with Isaac.

Explore

Rehoboth means "enough room." Plan a meal and invite some neighbors that you don't know very well. Make room for others by hosting them and getting to know them.

Jacob and Esau

Genesis 25:27–34; 27:1–28:5; 32:1–33:17

Connect
Both brothers needed to decide to forgive. Bless others with your willingness to say, "I'm sorry" or "I forgive you."

Isaac and Rebekah had twin sons, Esau and Jacob. Esau was the firstborn, so he had a birthright to an inheritance and blessing from their father.

The brothers grew up to like different things. Esau liked to hunt. Jacob liked to cook and stay close to the tent where they lived. One day, when Jacob was cooking lentil stew, Esau came in and said, "I am starving; give me some of that stew." Jacob said, "Give me your birthright and I will give you some stew." Esau was so hungry that he agreed and traded his birthright for some food.

Years later, their father Isaac was old and almost blind. He said to Esau, "Hunt and make me my favorite food. Then I will bless you before I die."

But Jacob got that blessing instead. While Esau was out, Rebekah—who liked Jacob best—prepared a special meal that Jacob took in to his father. He tricked Isaac into believing that he was his brother Esau. Isaac blessed him and said, "You shall rule over your brother. Many people will serve you."

When Esau returned, he went to his father, and said, "Here is your favorite food. Bless me, Father." Then Isaac realized that because he could not see he had blessed the wrong brother.

Esau wept bitterly. He was so angry that he thought about killing Jacob. Rebekah sent Jacob far away to keep him safe from Esau. Jacob married and became a very wealthy man.

Twenty years later, Jacob decided that he wanted to go home. As he and his family journeyed, he heard that his brother was coming towards them with four hundred people. Was Esau planning an attack?

Jacob sent Esau a present of hundreds of animals. When Jacob saw Esau, he bowed low. Esau ran to meet Jacob with outstretched arms, and Jacob cried, "Esau, seeing your face is like seeing God's face. Please accept my gift. God has blessed me."

So Esau accepted the gift from Jacob. After years of being apart, Esau and Jacob blessed each other with forgiveness and peace.

Wonder: How could Esau forgive his brother Jacob for what he had done?

Explore

Jacob gave his brother a gift to make peace with him. What gift can you give to make peace with a friend or family member?

35

Connect

Joseph told dreams that made his brothers angry. The brothers were jealous and punished Joseph. Reuben went along with some things, but also stood up to the others. What experiences can you relate to?

Joseph and his brothers

Genesis 37

Jacob had many children, but he loved Joseph best of all. When Joseph was seventeen years old, Jacob gave him a beautiful robe with long sleeves. Joseph's brothers were jealous.

One night Joseph had a strange dream. In the morning he told his brothers: "I dreamed we were all binding wheat sheaves in a field. Suddenly, my sheaf stood up and all of your sheaves bowed down." The brothers were angry. Was Joseph saying that he was better than they were?

Then Joseph had another dream. He said, "Last night I dreamed that the sun, moon, and eleven stars were bowing down to me." Even his father, Jacob, was surprised. He said, "What kind of a dream is that? Will your mother and I and your brothers bow down to you?"

Joseph's brothers took their flocks to a pasture far away. One day Jacob said to Joseph, "Go and check on your brothers and the flock. Then come and tell me how they're doing."

When Joseph's brothers saw him coming, some of them said, "Here comes the dreamer! Let's kill him and throw him into a pit." Reuben stood up to the others, saying, "Do not take his life. Throw him in the pit, but do not hurt him further."

When Joseph got to the pasture, his brothers snatched his robe and threw him into a pit. The brothers saw some traders passing by. Judah said, "Let's sell Joseph to the traders." They lifted Joseph out of the pit and sold him for twenty pieces of silver. The traders took Joseph to Egypt, where they sold him as a slave.

Reuben, who had left them for a while, returned to find Joseph gone. He tore his clothes out of grief and guilt. To hide what they had done, the brothers dipped Joseph's robe into blood from a goat. They took the robe to their father Jacob and said, "Look! This is what we found." Jacob said, "It's my son's robe! Joseph has died!" Jacob mourned for many days, and his sons and daughters could not comfort him.

Wonder: How would the story be different if Joseph had not told his brothers about his dreams?

Connect

Jacob sent many foods (like honey, pistachios, and almonds) as a gift to Joseph. What foods do you take to a party or family reunion?

Joseph forgives

Genesis 39–45

God was with Joseph while he was a slave in Egypt, even when he was wrongly sent to jail. There, Joseph explained the meaning of dreams to two of Pharaoh's workers. When Pharaoh himself had troubling dreams, one of those workers remembered Joseph. Pharaoh sent for Joseph and asked, "What do my dreams mean?"

In his first dream, Pharaoh was standing by the Nile River. Seven fat cows came out of the river. Then seven thin cows ate the fat cows. Next he dreamed about seven fat ears of grain that were swallowed by skinny ears of grain.

Joseph explained, "There will be seven good years, and then seven years of famine. Choose someone wise to be in charge of Egypt. Gather food and store it for the years of famine."

"You are very wise," said Pharaoh. Pharaoh placed his ring on Joseph's finger and put him in command.

Meanwhile, a famine came to Canaan where Joseph's family lived. Father Jacob said, "Go to Egypt to buy grain." All of his sons except young Benjamin left for Egypt.

When they got there, they bowed down to Joseph without knowing he was their brother. Joseph accused them of being spies and put them in jail. Then he released all but one of them on the condition that they would bring their younger brother to him.

When the brothers got back to Canaan, they told Jacob that they had to take Benjamin back with them. "No!" cried Jacob, "I won't lose Benjamin!" But the famine got worse. So Jacob told his sons, "Go to Egypt. May God be merciful. Take some food and money as a present to this man in Egypt."

Joseph organized a feast. The brothers bowed down and gave him gifts, but still did not recognize him. Finally, Joseph said, "Come closer to me. I am your brother Joseph. God has used me to keep many people alive. Bring our father and your families to live in Egypt."

Joseph hugged his brothers. The brothers returned to their father to tell him the news, "Your son is alive!" Jacob's family left Canaan and settled in Egypt.

Wonder: Show how you think the brothers looked when they found out that their brother Joseph was alive and a leader in Egypt.

Moses is born

Exodus 1:1–2:10

Connect
This story talks about courageous women. Who are some courageous women that you know?

Joseph and his brothers had many children. Their children had children and their children's children had children. Over time, Israelites filled the land. Egypt's new king, called Pharaoh, did not remember how Joseph's people had helped Egypt. He said, "There are too many Israelites—and they are too powerful. If we go to war, they will join our enemies and fight against us! We need a plan."

The Egyptians decided to wear down the people with work. Taskmasters forced the people to build cities for Pharaoh. They made them do every kind of field work. But the Israelites still multiplied and spread.

Pharaoh became so afraid that he even commanded people to kill the Israelites' baby boys. Two midwives named Shiphrah and Puah disobeyed the king and let baby boys live. Pharaoh angrily questioned them, but Shiphrah and Puah said, "There is nothing we can do! The Israelite women give birth before we even come to help them." Because of their courage, God blessed the two midwives.

When one Israelite mother had a beautiful baby boy, she hid him. But after three months, she could not hide him anymore. So she got a basket made of papyrus. She put the baby in the basket and placed it among the reeds on the riverbank. His sister stood nearby to watch over him and to see what happened.

Pharaoh's daughter came to the river to bathe. She saw the basket and sent her maid for it. When she opened the basket, she saw a crying baby, and she felt sorry for him. The baby's sister came up to the princess. "Shall I get you a nurse for the baby?" she bravely asked. "Yes," the princess replied.

The girl went and got her mother. Pharaoh's daughter said, "I will pay you to take this baby home and care for him." So the mother took her boy home again, and she was even paid to do it! When the child grew old enough, he went to live with Pharaoh's daughter, who adopted him and named him Moses.

Wonder: I wonder what it was like for Shiphrah and Puah to stand up to the Pharaoh.

Explore

The Hebrew word for basket in this story is the same word that is used for ark in the Noah story. What similarities do you see between this story of Moses and the story of Noah's ark?

41

Explore

God said, "I am who I am." There are many other names for God in the Bible like rock, fortress, eagle, refuge. The Hebrew word for the Lord is *Yahweh*. What words would you use to describe God?

42

Connect
Moses asked God many questions.
What questions do you like to ask God?

Moses and the burning bush

Exodus 2:23–3:22

The Israelites groaned under their slavery. They cried out and God heard them. God remembered the promises made to Abraham, Isaac, and Jacob.

Moses was taking care of his father-in-law's flock. He led them through the desert to a mountain. There, the angel of God appeared in a flame of fire out of a bush. The fire was blazing but the bush was not burning up.

Moses said, "I must step off the path and see this great sight."

When he walked toward the bush, God called, "Moses! Moses!"

"Here I am," Moses replied.

God said, "Come no closer! Take off your sandals, for this is holy ground. I am the God of Abraham, Isaac, and Jacob." And Moses hid his face, for he was afraid to look at God.

The Lord said, "I have seen the misery of my people and heard their cry. I have seen how badly the Egyptians treat them. I will free them and bring them to a good land. Come, I will send you to Pharaoh to bring my people out of Egypt."

But Moses said, "Who am I to do this?"

God said, "I will be with you."

Moses replied, "But what if they ask your name?"

God said, "I am who I am. Say to them, 'The God of your ancestors, the God of Abraham, Isaac, and Jacob has sent me to you.' Gather the leaders of the Israelites and tell them what I have told you. They will listen to you. But the king of Egypt will not willingly let you go. So I will strike Egypt with wonders. After that, Pharaoh will give in. And you will not go empty handed; you will leave with silver and gold jewelry and fine clothing."

Wonder: I wonder why God spoke to Moses from a burning bush.

Moses accepts God's call

Exodus 4

Connect

Do you ever feel that you don't have enough courage to do something? Challenge yourself to try something new. Trust that God will be with you and give you what you need.

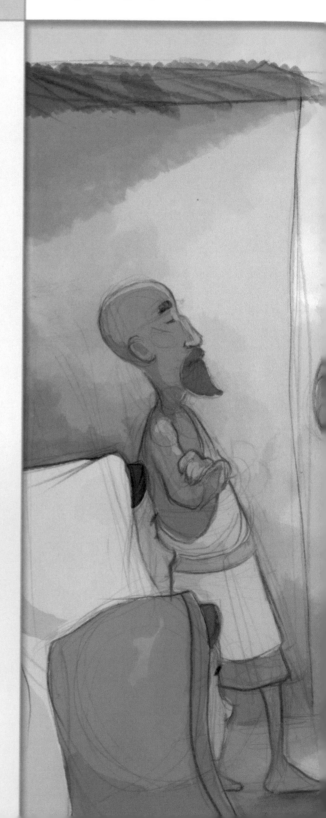

Moses listened as God spoke from the burning bush. Then Moses asked God, "What if the Israelites don't believe me?"

God replied, "What are you holding?"

"A staff," Moses answered.

"Throw it on the ground," God said. Moses threw it down, and the staff became a snake! Then God said, "Pick it up by the tail." Moses grabbed the tail and the snake became a staff again. God said, "This sign will help people believe that the God of their ancestors, the God of Abraham, Isaac, and Jacob appeared to you."

Then God said, "Put your hand inside your cloak." Moses obeyed. When he took his hand out, it had a skin disease and was as pale as snow. God said, "Put your hand back into your cloak." Moses did this and had a healthy hand again.

God said, "If people still will not believe, take water from the Nile River and pour it on the dry ground. It will become blood."

Moses said, "God, I have never been a good speaker." God replied, "Who gives the power to speak? Go. I will be with you and will teach you what to say."

But Moses pleaded, "Please send someone else." God was angry, but said, "Your brother Aaron can speak well. You will tell him what to say, and he will speak to the people for you."

So with his wife, Zipporah, and his sons, Moses left the land of Midian carrying God's staff. God said, "When you see Pharaoh, show him the signs I have taught you to perform. But even then Pharaoh will not let the people go right away."

God told Aaron to go into the wilderness to meet Moses. When they met, Moses told Aaron everything God had done. The two gathered the Israelite leaders, and Aaron spoke and performed all the signs. Everyone believed. When they heard that God had listened to them and sent help, they bowed down and worshiped.

Wonder: Why would the people need to see signs in order to believe Moses?

Explore

In this story, God turns the ordinary into the extraordinary. Do you know someone who with God's help has done something extraordinary?

Let my people go

Exodus 7:1–13:16

Explore

The yearly celebration of Passover recognizes God's power in bringing the Israelites out of Egypt. Read Matthew 26:17–30 to see how Jesus celebrated Passover with his disciples.

The Israelites continued to suffer as slaves. God told Moses and Aaron to go to Pharaoh and perform the signs God had given them. Aaron threw down his staff and it became a snake. He struck the Nile River and the water became blood. But, just as God had said, Pharaoh would not listen. He would not let the people go.

God sent Moses to tell Pharaoh that if he did not let the people go, frogs would cover the land. When this happened, Pharaoh asked Moses to pray for the frogs to go away and then he would let the Israelites go. But when the frogs went away, Pharaoh changed his mind.

Gnats flew everywhere, swarms of flies ruined the land, and diseases killed the animals. Painful sores covered the people's skin. But Pharaoh still would not listen. Thunder crashed, and hail smashed plants and trees. Locusts came and ate the green plants. Then Pharaoh said, "I have sinned. Pray to the Lord your God." But when the locusts left, Pharaoh did not let the Israelites go.

For three days Egypt was covered in darkness. Pharaoh called Moses and said, "Go, but leave your flocks and herds." Moses said, "Our animals go with us." Pharaoh got angry. Then Moses warned, "Every firstborn person and animal in Egypt will die." But Pharaoh refused to listen.

God told Moses what the Israelites should do. They were to put lamb's blood on their doorposts. They should roast the lamb and eat it with bitter herbs and flat, unleavened bread. They were to eat quickly, with their sandals on and their clothes ready for travel. God would pass through Egypt and protect those who obeyed.

At midnight, all the firstborn died in every unmarked home in Egypt. Pharaoh summoned Moses and Aaron and commanded, "Go worship your God. Take everything and go!"

The Israelites left immediately, taking their bread dough before it could rise. They left with gold, silver, and gifts of clothing.

Moses said, "Remember this day. Have a celebration every year, for God's mighty power has brought the people out of Egypt."

Wonder: I wonder why Pharaoh did not listen to Moses and Aaron. Why did Pharaoh keep changing his mind?

Connect

The Israelites had been in Egypt for hundreds of years! Jews and Christians continue to remember this story by sharing the Passover meal. Share matzo, a special Passover cracker, or other crackers and pray: *Thank you, God, for being faithful throughout the ages.*

Crossing the Red Sea

Exodus 13:17–15:21

Connect

Sing a song of praise with your family. Say a prayer of thanks to God for all of the ways God has led and blessed your family.

When Pharaoh let the Israelites go, God did not lead them straight through the nearest land, because they would have faced a war there. Instead God led them all around the wilderness toward the Red Sea. God went in front of them in a pillar of cloud by day. At night, God led them in a pillar of fire.

Meanwhile, Pharaoh and his officials said, "What have we done, losing our workers?!" Pharaoh took his army and hundreds of chariots. The Egyptians chased the Israelites and caught up to them as they camped by the sea.

The Israelites were very frightened and they cried out to God. They said to Moses, "It would have been better to serve the Egyptians than to die in the wilderness!" Moses replied, "Do not be afraid. Stand firm and trust God."

God said to Moses, "Tell the Israelites to go forward." The pillar of cloud moved behind the Israelites so that the Egyptians could not reach them that night.

Then Moses stretched out his hand over the sea. God sent a strong wind to drive the sea back and divide the waters. The Israelites went into the sea on dry ground, with the waters making a wall for them on their right and on their left.

The Egyptians followed the Israelites into the sea. But then Moses stretched his hand out over the sea again. The waters returned and covered Pharaoh's whole army.

The Israelites were finally free! They praised God. They sang these words:

The Lord is my strength and my might,
And he has become my salvation;
This is my God, and I will praise him . . .
The Lord will reign forever and ever.

Miriam, the sister of Moses and Aaron, took a tambourine and all the women went out after her with tambourines and with dancing. And Miriam sang to them, "Sing to the Lord, who has triumphed gloriously."

Wonder: Israelites celebrated God's victory. How would Egyptians have told this same story to their children?

Explore

Harriet Tubman was called "the Moses of her people." Learn about slavery in North America and the Underground Railroad that helped many escape to freedom. Find African-American spirituals that tell about this story from Exodus.

Explore

Manna means "What is it?" in Hebrew. Manna was white, like coriander seed, and tasted like honey-flavored wafers. Think of places in the world where people may need to eat the same food each day.

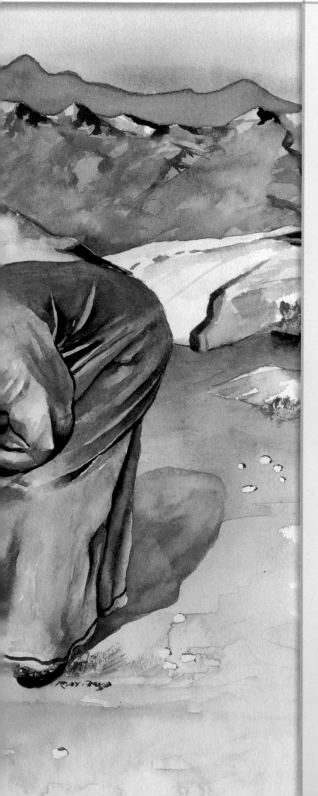

Connect

Talk about how you keep the Sabbath. Are there special things you can do together as a family to rest and have a different rhythm on one day of the week?

Enough food in the wilderness

Exodus 15:22–16:36

The people wandered in the wilderness for three days. They were very thirsty. The only water they could find tasted bitter. They grumbled, "What shall we drink?"

Moses cried out to God. God showed Moses a piece of wood. Moses threw it in the water and then the water tasted sweet. God said, "Listen to the voice of the Lord your God, and do what is right."

The people wandered in the wilderness for some more weeks. They became very, very hungry. They complained, "It would have been better to die in Egypt. At least there we had food to eat. Here in this wilderness we are going to die of hunger."

God told Moses, "I am going to rain bread from heaven for you. Every day the people should gather enough for that day, but no more. If they take too much, it will spoil. In the morning they will have bread, and in the evening they will have meat."

It happened just as God said. In the evenings, God provided small birds called quail to eat. In the mornings, God covered the ground with a flaky frost that looked like small seeds and tasted like wafers made with honey. Some people gathered what they needed, but others gathered more than enough, trying to save the food for the next day. That food became rotten and full of worms.

On the sixth day Moses told the people to gather twice as much food. This would feed them for that day and for the seventh day. Some people went out on the seventh day to gather food, but they found nothing. God had given them the seventh day, the Sabbath, for rest.

The Israelites called the bread manna. They ate it for forty years, until they came to the land of Canaan. God told the people to keep a jar of manna. That way, they could remember how God provided them with enough.

Wonder: Imagine traveling in a wilderness without having food to eat or clean water to drink.

52

Connect

What commandments are easy for you to follow? Which ones are hard? What ten commandments would you create to make your family's life peaceful and healthy?

Ten Commandments

Exodus 19:1–20:21

Three months after they left Egypt, the Israelites came to the wilderness of Sinai. They camped in front of the mountain. God called to Moses from the mountain, saying, "You have seen how I brought you to myself. Now if you obey my voice and keep my covenant, you will be my treasure."

Moses told the leaders what God had said. The people answered, "Everything that God has spoken we will do."

God said to Moses, "Go prepare the people. Tell them to wash their clothes and wait for me. On the third day, I will come down on the mountain. Tell the people not to go up on the mountain or touch it."

On the third morning, there was thunder and lightning. A thick cloud hid the mountain and a loud trumpet made everyone tremble. The people stood below the mountain. The trumpet grew louder and louder.

Moses spoke and God answered in thunder.

God called Moses to the top of the mountain.

Then God spoke all these words: "I am the Lord your God, who brought you out of the land of Egypt, out of the house of slavery; you shall have no other gods before me.

"You shall not make for yourself an idol.

You shall not misuse the name of the Lord your God.

Remember the Sabbath day, and keep it holy.

Honor your father and your mother.

You shall not murder.

Be faithful to your husband or wife.

You shall not steal.

You shall not tell lies about your neighbor.

You shall not covet your neighbor's house, or anything that belongs to your neighbor."

Moses gave all these words to the people. And the people witnessed the thunder and lightning, the sound of the trumpet, and the smoke on the mountain. They trembled and begged Moses to speak to God for them. Moses said, "Do not be afraid." He returned to the thick darkness above them to talk with God.

Wonder: I wonder if it was difficult for the Israelites to follow these rules.

Explore

Golden calves are mentioned again in 1 Kings 12:26–30. How are the two stories similar? Jeroboam was the first ruler of the Northern Kingdom after the kingdom of Israel split into two parts.

54

The golden calf

Exodus 24:12–18; 32:1–34:10

One day God said to Moses, "Come up to me on the mountain. I will give you tablets of stone with the law and the commandments written on them."

Moses left Aaron in charge of the people and went up the mountain. He was on the mountain for forty days and forty nights.

The people got tired of waiting for Moses to come back. They said to Aaron, "Come, make gods for us. They will go before us, since we do not know what has happened to Moses, the man who brought us up out of the land of Egypt."

Aaron told them, "Bring me all your gold earrings." He melted the earrings to make a statue of a calf. The people were excited and said, "This is our god!" They celebrated their new god by eating and drinking and dancing.

God became very angry. He said to Moses, "Go down at once! Your people have turned away from my commandments, and they are worshiping a golden calf." Moses went down from the mountain, carrying the two tablets with God's writing on them.

When he saw the calf and the dancing, Moses threw the tablets down and broke them. He burned the golden calf. Then he ground it to powder, scattered the powder onto water, and made the Israelites drink it.

Moses asked Aaron, "What have you done?"

Aaron replied, "Don't be angry! The people told me to make gods for them. I collected their gold jewelry, threw it into the fire, and out came this calf!"

Moses told the people, "You have acted very badly. But I will ask God to forgive you."

Moses went back up the mountain. God wrote the law on two new stone tablets.

God said, "I am a forgiving God. I am full of love. My love is not just for you but for your children and for your children's children."

Moses bowed his head and worshiped God.

Wonder: Why would the people want golden gods?

55

Celebrating the harvest

Leviticus 23:33–43; Deuteronomy 16:13–15

Connect
The Israelites were thankful that God provided for them in the wilderness. Keep a family journal of daily blessings.

Moses and the people lived in booths, or *sukkot*, as they journeyed through the wilderness.

After God brought them out of Egypt, God said to Moses, "Celebrate the Festival of Booths on the fifteenth day of the seventh month. Gather boughs of willows, leafy branches, and palm branches to make shelters. For seven days each year live in outdoor shelters to remember that I brought the people of Israel out of the land of Egypt.

"Rejoice together! You and your sons, daughters, slaves, strangers, orphans, and widows—everyone! Gather your harvest fruits and vegetables. Eat together and rejoice!"

So each year at the time of the harvest, the people celebrated. They gave offerings to God. They gathered boughs of willows, leafy branches, and palm branches and made shelters to remember that God was with the Israelite people in the wilderness.

Wonder: I wonder what it is like when everyone gathers to eat and celebrate together.

Explore

Jews still celebrate *Sukkot* by constructing shelters made of branches and telling this story. Part of this celebration includes showing hospitality. Invite someone to your house to celebrate that God is with you, even in hard times.

Jubilee

Leviticus 25:8–55

Connect
Many years later, Jesus proclaimed a Jubilee message. One Sabbath day, Jesus went to the synagogue and read from the book of Isaiah. He preached freedom, peace, and justice for everyone (Luke 4:16-20).

"Celebrate," God told Moses. "Sound the trumpets everywhere. Proclaim a year of Jubilee!"

People who had sold their land could celebrate. God said, "All the land will go back to its first owners in the year of Jubilee."

People who had sold their houses to buy food celebrated, too. God said, "In the year of Jubilee, give houses back to the families who owned them before."

People who were slaves also celebrated. God said, "Everyone is free in the year of Jubilee."

It was a fresh start for people and for the land. People were treated equally and everyone had enough. People cared for each other and for all of God's creation.

Wonder: I wonder why freedom is so important to God.

Explore

What if we would practice the year of Jubilee today? What would that look like? Who would give up land, and who would receive land? Who would be freed?

59

Explore
Be a spy and look for examples of God's trustworthy love around you. What do you notice?

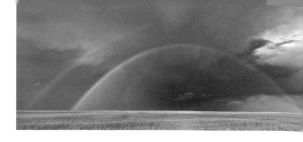

Connect
Fear can prevent us from trusting in God. Pray: *God, take my fear. I remember your promises and trust that you will help me.*

Moving toward Canaan

Numbers 13–14

When the Israelites were still in the wilderness, God told Moses to send some people to explore Canaan. This was the land that God had promised to the Israelites.

So Moses sent twelve spies to explore Canaan and find out what it was like.

The twelve spies traveled through Canaan for forty days. It was a beautiful place with plenty of water and good food. They found a bunch of grapes so big that two of the spies had to carry it on a pole! They also found that many people already lived in Canaan. These people were big and strong. They lived in cities with tall, strong walls.

When the twelve spies returned to Moses, ten of them were afraid. They said, "We cannot go into this land. The people there are too big and strong. They will fight us."

But two of the spies, Joshua and Caleb, remembered God's promise. They said, "This is a good land. God promised to give it to us. With God's help, we can go into this land."

But the people did not listen to Joshua and Caleb. Instead, they listened to the ten other spies. They were afraid to go into the land that God had promised them. They did not trust God to help them.

God told Moses, "Since the people did not believe my promise, I will not take them into this land. They will keep living in the wilderness. But I will not forget my promise. I will take their children into Canaan. Joshua and Caleb will also go because they trusted me."

The Israelites stayed in the wilderness for another forty years. The people were sad because they had not trusted God, but they knew that their children would enter the Promised Land some day.

Wonder: Caleb and Joshua trusted in God's promises. Why were ten spies fearful?

Explore

In the biblical world, words of judgment and curses were expected to bring bad things. In the same way, words of blessing would bring good things. How do you use your words to bless others?

Connect

Balaam listened to God's voice. Sit very quietly and take time to listen for God's still, small voice inside of you. What is God asking you to do?

Baalam, the donkey, and the angel

Numbers 22–24

The people of Moab were shaking in fear. The Israelites were camped near the land of Moab where Balak was king. King Balak called for his messengers and commanded them, "Find the prophet Balaam. Pay him to put a curse on the Israelite people who have come up from Egypt."

Balaam asked God what he should do. God answered, "These people are my people. They are blessed. Do not listen to Balak. When you go to these people, say only what I tell you."

Balaam left on his faithful donkey. Suddenly, the donkey saw an angel standing in the road, holding a sword. The donkey turned off the road and went into a field. Balaam hit the donkey to turn it back onto the road.

Later the donkey saw the angel again in a narrow path. It pressed against a wall to avoid the angel, and Balaam's foot scraped against the wall. Balaam struck the donkey again.

When the angel appeared a third time, the donkey sat down on the road. Balaam hit the donkey with his staff. God opened the mouth of the donkey and it said, "What have I done to you to make you hit me three times?"

Balaam said, "You have made a fool out of me!"

The donkey asked, "Do I usually behave like this?"

Balaam answered honestly, "No."

Then God let Balaam see the angel standing in the road with a sword in hand. Balaam bowed down so low that he fell on his face.

Balaam said, "Forgive me. I did wrong."

The angel told Balaam to listen and obey God. So, Balaam continued on his way to meet King Balak.

When he came before the king, Balaam said, "I am telling you only what God tells me to say. Anyone who blesses these people will be blessed. If you curse them, you will be cursed. God is with these people. They are God's people."

Wonder: I wonder why it took so long for Balaam to see the angel.

63

Explore

Exodus 25–27 and 35–40 give specific instructions for building the tent of meeting or tabernacle. Find a diagram of the tabernacle online or in a Bible reference book.

Connect

The five sisters recognized that a law was unfair and worked to change it. What do you notice that is unfair? What could you do to change it?

Sisters solve a problem

Numbers 27:1–11

The people of Israel belonged to different clans or families. Zelophehad, from the clan of Manasseh, died without having any sons. But he had five daughters. Their names were Mahlah, Noah, Hoglah, Milcah, and Tirzah.

The people were getting close to the land God had chosen for them to live in. The long wilderness journey was almost over. So the five daughters went to the entrance of the tent of meeting. They came to speak to Moses, Eleazar the priest, the leaders, and all the people gathered there.

The daughters said, "Our father has died. We are his children: Mahlah, Noah, Hoglah, Milcah, and Tirzah. He had no sons to inherit his land. Since he had no sons, let us have his land. Our father's name should be remembered. His name can continue through us."

Moses thought about their request and asked God what should be done. God said, "The daughters are right. Let them have land near their uncles. Tell the people that the new rule is: if a man dies without a son, they should give his things to his daughter."

Then Moses gave the decision. The daughters of Zelophehad should each be given their share of land. A new law was made for all the people of Israel. This was the command of God through Moses.

Wonder: I wonder why all five sisters went to talk to Moses.

Explore

Find out about the *mezuzah*, a piece of parchment paper inscribed with these verses from Deuteronomy. The paper is rolled up, placed in a case, and the case is attached to the doorpost of the home.

Some Jews wear *tefillin* on their arms or fore-heads to remind them of this passage from Deuteronomy about loving God with heart, soul, and might. What reminds you to love God?

Love the Lord

Deuteronomy 6:1–13

The Israelite people looked forward to living in Canaan, a land flowing with rich milk and sweet honey. Moses spoke to the Israelite people,

"Listen to these commandments from the Lord your God. If you want to live well in the land that you are entering, listen!

"Hear, O Israel: the Lord is our God, the Lord alone.

"Love the Lord your God with all your heart, and with all your soul, and with all your might.

"Keep these words that I am commanding you today in your heart.

"Recite them to your children. Talk about them when you are at home and when you are away, when you lie down and when you rise.

"Write these words on your hands and on your fore-heads to remember them. Write them on the doorposts of your house and on your gates.

"When you are in this beautiful land that God prom-ised to Abraham, Isaac, and Jacob, be careful that you do not forget God. When you have beautiful houses, when you have bountiful crops to harvest and eat, when you have large, prosperous cities, when you have eaten until you are full, do not forget God. Do not forget the Lord your God who brought you out of slavery in Egypt."

Wonder: Imagine the people loving God with every bit of themselves—heart, soul, and might.

Promised Land dreams

Deuteronomy 30, 34

Connect

Pray: *God, give me courage to choose life and the ways that are pleasing to you.*

The Israelites spent many years in the wilderness with Moses as their leader. They were no longer slaves but they had not reached the land of their ancestors. Near the end of his days, Moses gave a speech. He shared God's promise of a homeland where they could live.

"If you and your children obey God with all your heart then God will have mercy on you. Even if you are scattered to the ends of the earth, God will gather you together again. God will bring you to the land where your ancestors lived, and you will live there and prosper.

"When you turn to God with all your heart and soul, you will succeed in everything you do. You will have many children, large herds of livestock, and healthy crops."

Moses went on to say, "See, today you may choose life or death. You can obey God's commandments by loving God and walking in God's ways. If you do this, then you will live. You will have many children and your children will have many children. God will bless you in the land that you are entering."

"But," Moses warned, "if you turn away from God, you will lose this land. So, choose life! Then you and your children and grandchildren may live in the land that God gave to your ancestors, to Abraham, Isaac, and Jacob."

When Moses finished his speech, he blessed the people. Then he went up from the plains of Moab to Mount Nebo. From that high place, God showed him the whole land and said, "This is the land that I promised to Abraham, Isaac, and Jacob. I have let you see it, but you will not cross over there."

Then Moses, the servant of God, died and was buried there in the land of Moab. He was one hundred twenty years old. The people wept and mourned for thirty days.

Never again was there a prophet like Moses. He spoke to God face to face, and performed many signs and wonders. He was a true leader of his people.

Wonder: I wonder if the Israelite people chose life and obedience to God.

Explore

Canaan, the Promised Land, was a land of fertile fields and olive groves. Pomegranates, figs, nuts, dates, grapes, and vegetables grew in that warm climate. Find out what foods are grown in Israel/Palestine today.

God calls Joshua

Joshua 1:1–17

Connect

God promised to stay with Joshua to give him courage. In what situations do you need courage? Think of words you can pray at those times.

Before Moses died God instructed him to call Joshua to be the new leader of the Israelites. Moses laid his hands on Joshua, and because of this Joshua was full of wisdom.

After Moses died God spoke to Joshua and told him that it was time to cross the Jordan River into Canaan. This was the land God had promised to the Israelites as their new home. It was a large territory, stretching from the Jordan River to the Great Sea.

God said, "As I was with Moses I will be with you. I will not fail you or abandon you. Be strong and courageous and bring the people to their new homeland."

God said again: "Be strong and courageous. Follow all Moses's instructions. Don't turn from the laws Moses gave you. If you don't turn to the right or to the left, you will succeed wherever you go. Think about the law always, during the day and at night, and you will succeed wherever you go."

God said a third time: "I command you, Joshua, to be strong and courageous. Do not be frightened for I am with you wherever you go."

So Joshua told the people, "Get ready, because in three days you will cross the Jordan River. God will give us land there. It will be our new home."

Wonder: "Be strong and courageous." Why do you suppose God repeated the same words so many times?

Explore

The Israelites had wandered as refugees. Learn more about refugees who have come to live in your country.

1

Crossing the Jordan

Joshua 3–4

Connect

Set up a memorial stone inside or outside your house to remind you of a time that God did something amazing.

Joshua led the Israelites to the Jordan River. This was at harvest time when the river was so full that it overflowed its banks. The Israelites spent three days getting ready to cross the rushing river.

Joshua told the people, "Get ready! We haven't come this way before, so when you see the ark of the covenant, follow it. God will do amazing things!" The priests set out with the ark, and the people followed.

As the priests stepped into the water, the water stopped flowing. All the water stood up in a heap and left a dry riverbed where the priests were standing. The priests carried the ark into the middle of the riverbed. They stayed there while all the people crossed over on dry ground.

God said to Joshua, "Call twelve men, one from each tribe. Have them take twelve stones from the riverbed and set them down in the place where you camp tonight." Joshua called the people and they did what he told them.

As soon as all the people had crossed over, the priests followed, carrying the ark of the covenant. As soon as their feet touched the land on the other side, the river started flowing again.

The stone carriers set up the twelve stones at Gilgal where the Israelites camped that night. Joshua said to the people, "Soon your children will ask, 'What do these stones mean?' Then you can tell them what God has done. You can say, 'God dried up the waters so that we could walk across this river. These stones help us remember the greatness of God. We will remember and honor God forever.'"

Wonder: Find the twelve stones in the picture. Why do you think there were twelve?

Explore

The crossing of the Jordan took place when the river was at flood stage. That is the most difficult time to cross any river. What story in Exodus does this remind you of?

75

Explore

The ark of the covenant was a chest made of acacia wood and covered with gold. It was the symbol of God's presence. Look for pictures online to see how it might have looked.

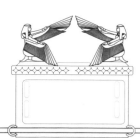

Connect

Tie a piece of yarn around your wrist to remember to pray for people who might be your enemies.

Rahab and Jericho's walls

Joshua 2, 6

The Israelites traveled until they were near the city of Jericho. Joshua sent two spies into the city. They went to the house of a young woman named Rahab. She knew they were Israelites, but she welcomed them into her home.

The king of Jericho heard about the spies and sent soldiers to Rahab's house.

"Quick!" Rahab said. "The soldiers are looking for you. Go hide on my roof." She hid the spies under stalks of flax. She told the soldiers that the spies had gone away, and the soldiers hurried off after them.

Then Rahab went back to the spies and said, "I know God has given you this land. I have heard how God parted the Red Sea. Your God is God in heaven above and on earth below."

She let the spies down the city wall with a rope from her window. They said to her, "Tie this red cord to your window. You and all your family will be safe when we come to take your city."

God instructed Joshua, "The city will be yours. For six days, you must march in silence around the city. Seven priests will walk behind you carrying the ark of the covenant. The rest of the priests will carry trumpets. On the seventh day, everyone will walk around the city seven times. Then the priests will blow their trumpets and everyone will shout."

The people did what Joshua said, and when the priests blew their trumpets on the seventh day, Joshua said, "Shout! God has given us the city."

The people shouted and Jericho's walls came crashing down. The Israelites went into Jericho and took it over. The Israelites kept the promise the spies had made and did not harm Rahab. She and her family were kept safe and came to live with the Israelites.

Wonder: I wonder why Rahab, who was a foreigner to the Israelites, chose to help the spies.

Gideon

Judges 6:1–7:23

Connect
Have there been times that you have wished for a sign that God was with you?

An angel of God came to Gideon and said, "God is with you. God is sending you to save the Israelites from the Midianites."

But Gideon said, "How can I do that? I am the weakest in my tribe and in my family. I need a sign. Show me that it's really God who is speaking to me."

Gideon brought meat and bread outside and placed them on a rock. The angel's staff touched the food. Fire sprang up from the rock and burned up the food. The angel disappeared. Then Gideon knew God had spoken to him.

But later, Gideon said to God, "Are you really going to use me to save the people? I need a sign. In the morning, please make this piece of sheep's wool wet with dew. Make the ground around it dry." And God did that.

Then Gideon said, "I need one more sign. In the morning, make the sheep's wool dry, and all the ground around it wet." And God did that as well. Then Gideon knew God would use him to save the people.

The Midianites had a huge army, so Gideon gathered a huge army too. God said, "Gideon, your army is too big. If you win this battle, the people will not say, 'God is strong.' They will say, 'Israel is strong.' Send home the men who are scared."

Twenty-two thousand soldiers went home. Then there were ten thousand.

Again, God said, "The army is too big. Take them down to the water for a drink." Gideon did. Then God said, "Send home all the soldiers who kneel down to drink." When Gideon did, only three hundred were left.

Gideon gave each of those soldiers a trumpet and a torch. At Gideon's command, the soldiers blew their trumpets and shouted, "For the Lord and for Gideon." When the Midianite army saw the torches and heard the great sound, they turned and ran away. The Israelites were safe.

Wonder: I wonder why God chose Gideon, who was the weakest in his family.

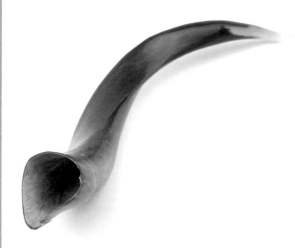

Explore
The trumpets used by Gideon's army were *shofars*, a wind instrument made from animal horns. The shofar called people to battle and also announced the Sabbath. Listen to shofar sounds online.

Ruth and Naomi

Ruth 1–4

Naomi and her husband Elimelech lived in Judah, in the city of Bethlehem. They had two sons. When famine came to the land and there was not enough food, the family moved to the country of Moab.

Elimelech died in Moab, but their sons grew up and got married. One son married a woman named Ruth. The other married a woman named Orpah. Then both of Naomi's sons died. Naomi, Ruth, and Orpah were left without their husbands.

Naomi decided to return to Bethlehem. She said to Ruth and Orpah, "You must each go back to your mother's house. You have been very kind to me. May God also be kind to you. I hope you will both marry again and have children."

Orpah wept and kissed Naomi; then she went on her way. But Ruth said to Naomi, "Do not make me leave you. Where you go, I will go. Where you live, I will live. Your people will be my people, and your God will be my God."

Together, Naomi and Ruth went to Bethlehem. It was the time of harvest so every day Ruth worked in the fields of a man named Boaz. She brought home grain and shared it with Naomi.

Boaz made sure no one bothered her. He gave her food and drink.

"Why are you helping me?" Ruth asked. "I am from a faraway land."

"You have been kind to Naomi," said Boaz. "May God also be kind to you."

Later, Boaz and Ruth were married. Ruth had a baby boy named Obed. The women in the town said to Naomi, "God has been so kind to you. You lost your sons, but now you have Ruth who loves you, and baby Obed to care for. Blessed be the Lord."

Wonder: I wonder why Ruth wanted to go with Naomi instead of returning to the house of her mother.

Connect

Boaz was very kind to Ruth and Naomi by offering food from his land. How can we show kindness to strangers from other places?

Sharing the harvest

Ruth 2

Explore

Gleaning is still done today to feed hungry people and to keep food from going to waste. Search for a gleaning project near you.

When Ruth moved with Naomi to Bethlehem, it was the harvest season. Ruth said to Naomi, "Let me go to the field and glean barley behind the workers." Naomi said, "Go, my daughter."

So Ruth went to the field belonging to a rich man named Boaz and gleaned barley behind the harvesters.

On the day Ruth began gleaning, Boaz came to the field and greeted the workers. He saw Ruth and asked, "Who is this young woman?"

A worker told him, "She is from Moab. She and her mother-in-law, Naomi, need food to eat. She has been working from early in the morning until now, and she has not rested even for a moment."

Boaz went to Ruth and spoke kindly to her: "Stay in my field and glean near my young women. I have told my young men not to bother you. When you are thirsty, you may drink water from our water jars."

Ruth bowed down with her face to the ground. She asked, "Why are you being so kind to me? I am a stranger in this land."

Boaz answered, "I have heard about you. After your husband's death, you cared for your mother-in-law and left your homeland. May God bless you for the good things you have done. May you be rewarded by the God of Israel, whose wings are sheltering you."

Boaz offered Ruth bread and wine vinegar at meal-time. He also gave her some roasted grain. Ruth ate until she was full.

When Ruth went back to gleaning, Boaz told his workers to leave even more grain for her. That evening, Naomi was surprised to see how much grain Ruth had gathered. Naomi said, "May God bless Boaz for his kindness."

Ruth continued to glean in Boaz's fields. Boaz protected her and she gathered barley and wheat until the end of the harvest season. She and Naomi lived together and had enough to eat.

Wonder: Imagine traveling to a strange land and having no food to eat.

Explore

Samuel's call came before the lamp of God had gone out (1 Samuel 3:3). Light stands for God's presence in the darkness. Read Exodus 25:31–40 for a description of the temple lampstand.

Connect

Eli was Samuel's mentor and teacher. Who teaches you about God?

The call of Samuel

1 Samuel 1–3

Hannah and her husband Elkanah wanted a baby very much. They had waited year after year. One year when Hannah went to the yearly worship celebration at Shiloh she prayed, "Please God, remember me." Then she made a promise: "If you give me a son, I'll dedicate him to serve you for his whole life."

Eli, the temple priest, saw Hannah praying. "Go in peace. The God of Israel will grant your petition."

Within the next year Hannah and Elkanah had a son, whom they named Samuel. When Samuel was six years old, Hannah took him to the temple. This time Hannah prayed, "My heart rejoices in the Lord. There is no Holy One like the Lord, no one besides you; there is no Rock like our God."

Then Samuel stayed at the temple to prepare to serve God. The priest Eli cared for Samuel and taught him the ways of God.

One night Samuel suddenly woke up as a voice called, "Samuel, Samuel." Thinking Eli was calling him, Samuel said, "Here I am" as he ran to Eli. Eli, who hadn't called Samuel, told him to go back to bed.

Again Samuel woke up hearing, "Samuel, Samuel!" Again he ran to Eli calling, "Here I am!" Eli sent Samuel back to bed a second time. Still, Samuel thought he heard Eli calling, "Samuel, Samuel!" and again ran to Eli saying, "Here I am!" This time, Eli told Samuel that it must be God calling.

The next time Samuel heard the voice calling, "Samuel, Samuel!" he answered as Eli instructed: "Speak, for your servant is listening."

God said to Samuel, "Eli's sons are not following my ways. There will be great trouble for them and for Eli."

In the morning, Samuel was afraid to tell Eli what God had said. But Eli said, "Do not hide God's words from me." So Samuel told him everything. Eli accepted God's message even though it was sad news.

Samuel continued to serve God at the temple. God was with Samuel and blessed the words he spoke.

Wonder: How did Eli know that it was God calling Samuel?

83

Saul becomes king

1 Samuel 8:1–10:25

Connect
Imagine someone saying, "God has chosen YOU!"

When Samuel grew old, he made his sons judges over Israel. But they did not follow God's ways and the people said, "Give us a king to rule over us, so that we can be like other nations."

Samuel warned against this, but they insisted. God said, "Do as the people ask. I will send you a man from the land of Benjamin. You will anoint him to be the king of Israel."

Kish was a man of Benjamin. One day, his donkeys strayed and he sent his son Saul to look for them. Saul's servant suggested, "Let's go to town and see if the prophet Samuel can tell us where the donkeys are."

On the way to town, they met Samuel, but did not know him. "Can you tell us where to find the prophet Samuel?" they asked. Right then, God told Samuel, "This is the one I have chosen to rule over the people." Samuel said to Saul, "Your donkeys are safe. Come with me. You are the one the people have been looking for."

"Me?" said Saul. "I am from the tribe of Benjamin, the smallest tribe of Israel. And my family is the least important one in the tribe. Why are you saying this to me?"

The next morning, Samuel anointed Saul by pouring oil on his head. "God has anointed you king over Israel. You will save the people from their enemies. Now God will show you some signs. First two men will tell you that the donkeys have been found and that your father is worried about you. Next you will meet three men who will give you two loaves of bread. Then you will meet people who are playing harps, tambourines, flutes, and lyres. When these things happen, you will know that God is with you."

Everything happened just as Samuel had said. Later, Samuel gathered all the people. He brought Saul's tribe forward. But Saul was not there! They looked and looked, and finally found him hiding among the baggage. Samuel called Saul forward and said, "Saul is the one who will be king."

Wonder: I wonder why Saul was chosen since he was from the smallest, least important tribe of Israel.

Map of Israel
The Twelve Tribes

Great Sea

DAN
ASHER
NAPHTALI
ZEBULUN
ISSACHAR
WEST MANASSEH
EAST MANASSEH
EPHRAIM
GAD
BENJAMIN
DAN   Jerusalem   REUBEN
Dead Sea
JUDAH
SIMEON

Explore

The twelve tribes of Israel were named after the sons of Jacob. Joseph's two sons, Ephraim and Manasseh also became heads of tribes. Compare the list in Exodus 1 to the lists in Numbers 1.

Samuel anoints David

1 Samuel 16:1–13

Connect

Think of your friends and family members. What good qualities does each person have that might surprise others?

Samuel was God's prophet. Samuel had anointed Saul as king but Saul had not been a good ruler. So God told Samuel it was time to choose a new king. God said, "Take some anointing oil and go to Jesse's house in Bethlehem. I have chosen one of his sons to be the next king."

Samuel said, "If Saul hears that I have anointed a new king, he will kill me."

God told him, "Take a young cow with you and say, 'I have come to make a sacrifice to God.' Invite Jesse and his sons to the sacrifice. I will tell you which son to anoint as king."

So Samuel went to Bethlehem and invited Jesse and his sons to the sacrifice. Jesse brought his oldest son before Samuel. Samuel looked at him and thought, "This must be the one who will be king." But God said to Samuel, "Do not look at his height or his appearance. I do not look at people the way you do. You see the way he looks. I see his heart."

Jesse brought his second son before Samuel. God said, "This is not the one I have chosen." And so it went. Jesse brought seven sons before Samuel. But God did not choose any of them to be king.

Samuel said to Jesse, "Are all your sons here?" Jesse replied, "My youngest son is not here. He is out watching the sheep." "Bring him at once," said Samuel.

So they brought David, the youngest son, before Samuel. God said to Samuel, "Anoint David, for he is the one."

Samuel did as God said. He anointed David, and God's spirit came to David. David would become the next king of Israel.

Wonder: I wonder what God saw in David that would help make him a good king.

David trusts God

1 Samuel 17

Connect

David trusted that God would help him. Pray together: *God, help me to trust that you are with me, especially when I am afraid or feeling small. Amen.*

Once, while Saul was still king, the Philistines challenged the Israelites to battle. The two armies stood on the sides of two mountains, facing each other, with a valley in between.

Goliath was a huge man and a Philistine champion. He dared the Israelites, "Send someone to fight me. If he wins, we will be your servants. If I win, you will be our servants." These words frightened the Israelites. No one wanted to fight Goliath.

Three of David's brothers were soldiers in Saul's army. One day, David's father told him to leave his sheep and take a lunch of bread and cheese to his brothers. David heard Goliath shouting, just as he had for the past forty days, "Give me a man to fight."

David said, "Who is this man, who insults our army and the living God?" This made David's brother Eliab angry. "Why did you leave your sheep? You have just come to watch the battle."

But King Saul heard about David's words and sent for him. David told Saul, "Let no one be afraid. I will go and fight him."

Saul said, "You? You are just a boy! How can you fight him?"

David replied, "I have kept sheep for my father. Whenever a lion or a bear came and attacked a lamb, I rescued the lamb from its mouth. God has saved me from lions and bears. Surely God will save me from this man who has insulted the living God."

So Saul said, "Go and may God be with you." He would have given his own armor to David, but David could not wear it. He went to fight Goliath with just a sling and five smooth stones.

Goliath mocked David for coming with only a sling. But David replied, "You have come to me with weapons, but I come to you in the name of the living God."

Goliath walked toward David. David quickly slung a stone at Goliath. The stone hit Goliath's forehead, and huge Goliath fell to the ground. Goliath was defeated and the Philistines ran away in fear.

Wonder: Why was David the only one not afraid to accept Goliath's challenge?

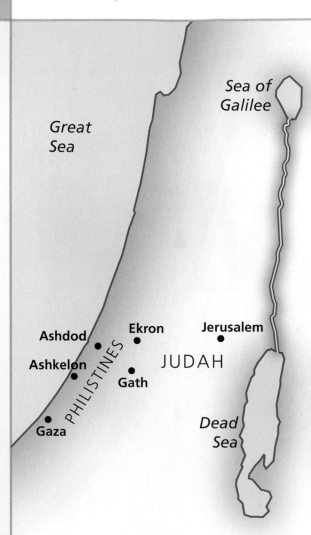

Explore

The Philistines were a constant threat to the Israelites. They lived in five cities: Ashdod, Ashkelon, Ekron, Gath, and Gaza. Find these cities on the map of Palestine in the time of the judges.

Connect

Both Jonathan and Michal acted with great courage. Pray: *God, give me boldness to help others.*

Explore

Being a good friend sometimes takes courage. What can you do to stand up for your friends and help them in hard times?

David and Jonathan

1 Samuel 18–20

King Saul was so pleased with David for defeating Goliath that he brought David to live in his own palace. As they returned home, women came out of the towns to sing and dance because of the victory. They praised Saul, but they praised David even more. This did not make the king happy.

Saul's son, Jonathan, met David and they became friends. The two of them made a covenant with each other and Jonathan gave David many gifts. Other Israelites also loved David because he was a hero. He was successful in everything he did.

The king began to worry that the people liked David better than they liked him. He could see that God was with David. A terrible idea formed in Saul's heart. He decided to kill David.

King Saul told his son, Jonathan, what he was going to do. But because Jonathan loved David, he ran to warn David of his father's plan. David left the palace and hid in a field.

Jonathan bravely spoke to his father. He said, "Don't kill David. You know that he is a good man. He has helped all of Israel!" Because of Jonathan's courage, King Saul changed his mind. He allowed David to return to the palace.

But once again, King Saul became jealous and wanted to hurt David. This time David's wife Michal bravely helped him escape through a palace window. David ran away, and King Saul was furious.

David found Jonathan and asked, "What have I done to your father? Why is he trying to kill me?" This time they knew that David would have to go far away to get away from Saul. The two friends, who loved each other dearly, cried when they had to say goodbye. Jonathan said to David, "Go in peace. We have promised to keep each other safe and even to help each other's families. Go in peace."

Wonder: Imagine what it was like for Jonathan to speak up to his father, the king.

Abigail prevents war

1 Samuel 25:1–35

Connect
Sometimes we may need to apologize, even when we didn't mean to hurt someone. You can say, "I'm sorry," when you hurt a friend's feelings. You may even want to offer them some food like Abigail did!

David stayed far away as long as Saul remained king of Israel. David and his soldiers were hiding in the wilderness near the home of Nabal, a rich but selfish man who owned many goats and sheep. David's soldiers often made sure that Nabal's shepherds and sheep were safe.

One day, Nabal was giving a feast. David sent some of his soldiers to Nabal to say, "Peace be to you, and peace be to your house, and peace be to all that you have. We have helped your shepherds. May we share in your food and drink?"

Nabal said, "Who is this David? Why should I give bread and meat to people I don't even know?"

The soldiers returned and told David what Nabal had said. David was very angry. "We helped him and now he is insulting us. Strap on your swords," he said.

Nabal was married to a woman named Abigail, who was clever and kind. One of Nabal's shepherds quickly went to Abigail. He said, "David and his soldiers were good to us, but our master shouted insults at them. Now they are coming to fight us."

Abigail quickly made a plan. She loaded food onto her donkeys: five sheep ready to roast, two hundred loaves of bread, two skins of wine, one hundred clusters of raisins, two hundred fig cakes, and some grain. She sent servants ahead of her with the food. She followed behind on a donkey.

When Abigail saw David, she got off her donkey and bowed down to the ground. "Please let me speak to you," she said. "I did not hear your soldiers asking Nabal for food. He has acted selfishly. But please accept this gift of food and do not let your anger turn to fighting."

David replied, "Blessed be God, and blessed be your good sense! God sent you to me, Abigail. Blessed be God, who kept me from hurting you and from being hurt." He accepted Abigail's gifts and said, "Go home in peace. I have heard your words and I will do what you said. I will not fight."

Wonder: Imagine how Abigail felt as she was on her way to meet David.

Explore

Sometimes peacemaking requires quick thinking, like Abigail did. It also may require accepting an apology and changing a plan, like David did. Can you think of any situations where you can make peace?

Connect

David showed great kindness to Mephibosheth. Try to show great kindness to someone this week.

David begins his rule

2 Samuel 7, 9

After King Saul's death, David was anointed king over Israel. David captured the city of Jerusalem and brought the ark of the covenant there. He made the city his capital. Then David thought, "I have a fine house but the ark of the covenant is in a tent. I should build a house for God."

But the prophet Nathan came to David and said, "God did not ask for a house of cedar. God lives and moves wherever the people are. But God makes this promise to you, that one of your sons will build the temple and your kingdom will last for generations."

David spoke to God. He said, "You are great, O God. There is no one like you and there is no God beside you. Thank you for your promise. Please bless me and bless my family forever."

King David ruled all Israel with justice and fairness. Although King Saul had tried to kill him, he called a servant to him and asked, "Is there anyone in Saul's family still alive? I want to show kindness to them because of my love for Jonathan, Saul's son."

The servant, Ziba, said, "Yes, a son of Jonathan is still alive. His name is Mephibosheth. He is lame in both his feet and cannot walk very well."

David called Jonathan's son to his palace, and Mephibosheth bowed down low before him. David said, "Do not be afraid. Your father was my good friend, and I will show you kindness for his sake. I will return to you all the land that belonged to your grandfather Saul, and I want you to eat at my table."

Then David called the servant Ziba to him and said, "I have given Saul's land to his grandson. I want you and your family to farm those fields so that Mephibosheth's whole family will have plenty of food." Ziba answered, "My lord king, I will do everything you command."

So Ziba and his family farmed the lands of Mephibosheth. But Mephibosheth lived in Jerusalem and ate at the king's table for the rest of his life.

Wonder: I wonder why David wanted to build a house for God.

Nathan confronts King David

2 Samuel 11:1–12:15

Explore

David was a powerful king. The prophet Nathan confronted the king by telling a powerful story. Think of other stories that help people do the right thing.

There are many stories of King David's courage and kindness. This is a story of a time King David did wrong.

David saw a woman named Bathsheba and wanted to be with her. But Bathsheba was already married to Uriah, a soldier in his army. So David came up with a terrible plan. He sent Uriah into the front of a battle, hoping that he would be killed. And David's wish came true. Uriah fought in the battle and was killed. Then David brought Bathsheba to his palace and married her.

God was not pleased by this, and sent the prophet Nathan to David. Nathan told David a story. He said:

"Once upon a time there lived a man who was very rich. He had a huge flock of sheep.

"In that same town, there lived a poor man. He owned only one thing: a little lamb. This lamb grew up with him and with his children. She ate the same food they ate. She even slept next to the man at night. The man loved the little lamb like she was his own child.

"One day a traveler came to visit the rich man. The rich man wanted to make a feast for the traveler. He was a greedy man and didn't want to use one of his many sheep. So he took the poor man's one little lamb."

When King David heard this story, he was very angry. He said, "That rich man deserves to die because he had no pity and took the poor man's one lamb. He must give the poor man four lambs to replace the one lamb he took."

Nathan looked at King David and said, "You are that man! God anointed you king and gave you everything you needed. Uriah and Bathsheba had only each other and their happiness together. You wanted Bathsheba and so you sent Uriah to die. You took what little Uriah had. You did it secretly but now everyone in the kingdom will know."

King David covered his face with his hands, "I have sinned against God." Nathan said, "Because you are truly sorry, God forgives you—but that cannot change everything. Some sad things will happen because of what you've done."

Wonder: Why did King David want more, when he had so much already?

Connect

Look around your house. Do you have just enough, or more than enough? It's natural to want more. We can pray that God will help us to be content with enough, and not always yearn for more.

97

Building the temple

1 Kings 6, 8

King Solomon, son of David, began to build a great temple in Jerusalem. God said to Solomon, "If you walk in my ways and obey my laws, I will be with you and the people of Israel." So Solomon made the temple as big and beautiful as he could.

The temple was made of stone, three stories tall. It had porches all around and winding staircases to each level. The floors, doors, roof, and ceiling were made of sweet-smelling wood like cedar and olivewood. Skilled artisans carved flowers, palm trees, and cherubim into the wood. Much of the inside was overlaid in gold. There was an inner sanctuary, the most holy place—a special room just for the ark of the covenant.

It took seven years to build the temple. When it was finished, Solomon invited many people to a dedication ceremony. The priests brought the ark from the old tent of meeting where people used to worship. They carried it into the temple and into the inner sanctuary. When the priests came out of the holy place, a cloud filled the temple and the glory of God filled God's house.

After Solomon blessed the people, he spread out his hands to the heavens and said, "O Lord, God of Israel, there is no God like you in heaven above or on earth beneath, keeping covenant and steadfast love for your servants who walk before you with all their heart. Will God live on earth? No! Will God live in a house? No! Even heaven cannot hold you, God."

Then Solomon prayed for the people who would come to worship God at the temple. He prayed for the land, for the people of the land, and even for people from other lands. "O God, answer whatever prayers and needs each person brings, for only you know what is in every human heart."

Then all the people worshiped together and celebrated for seven days. On the eighth day, they blessed the king and joyfully returned to their tents, grateful for God's goodness.

Wonder: Imagine worshiping and celebrating together for seven days in a beautiful, new temple.

Explore

Look up the Duomo Cathedral in Florence, Italy, and the Notre Dame Cathedral in Paris, France, for examples of beautiful cathedrals that took one hundred to two hundred years to construct.

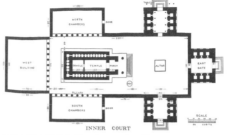

**Floor plan of
Solomon's temple**

Explore

There are many ways to be wise. In which area do you show wisdom: knowing about nature, relationships between people, knowing about God? You may also show wisdom while playing sports, doing math, or playing music.

Solomon's wisdom and folly

1 Kings 3–11

King Solomon was remembered by the people for doing both good and bad things. When he remembered God, he acted wisely. When he forgot God, he acted foolishly.

When Solomon first became king, he had a dream. In his dream, God said, "What would you like me to give you?"

Solomon answered, "God, even though I am young, you have made me king after my father, David. Give me an understanding mind. Make me able to judge what is good and what is evil, so that I can be a good king for your people."

God said, "You could have asked for riches and honor. Instead you asked for understanding to know what is right. If you walk in my ways, you will have wisdom. With your wisdom, you will receive riches, honor, and a long life."

People were amazed by Solomon's wisdom. In one argument two women both claimed to be the mother of the same baby. Solomon figured out a way to tell which woman was the true mother and gave the baby back to her.

Solomon understood trees and birds and animals and fish. He wrote many sayings and songs. People traveled from all over to listen to him. Even the queen of Sheba came from far away to test him with hard questions. Solomon could explain everything she asked. The queen said, "You are even wiser than I had heard. Blessed be God who has made you king of Israel."

But then Solomon began to turn away from God's ways. He got rich by making people work without pay. Solomon had many wives, the daughters of kings from nearby countries. He built temples for other gods and worshiped other gods. One of his wives was the daughter of an Egyptian pharaoh. Like the king of Egypt, he gathered many horses and chariots and a large army even though God said not to.

God said to Solomon, "Since you have not followed my commandments, I will take this kingdom away from you."

Solomon ruled in Israel for forty years. When he died, he was buried in Jerusalem.

Wonder: I wonder why Solomon changed and stopped walking in God's ways.

Explore

Your family can help people in your neighborhood by collecting food for a local food bank or inviting people to your house for a meal.

102

Elijah and the miracle of enough

1 Kings 17:1–16

After Solomon died, the kingdom was divided. Israel was in the north and Judah was in the south. Many kings did not follow God's ways. Prophets spoke truth to the kings. Elijah, in the northern kingdom of Israel, was one of these prophets.

The prophet Elijah went to see King Ahab with a message: "As surely as God lives, there will be no rain."

Then God spoke to Elijah, "Leave this area, Elijah. Hide near the wadi, the riverbed on the other side of the Jordan River. I will give you fresh water to drink and ravens will bring you meat and bread to eat."

Elijah obeyed God. He lived by the wadi on the other side of the Jordan River. Just as God had said, ravens brought him food and he drank water from the wadi. But eventually the wadi dried up because there was no rain. Then God spoke to Elijah again, saying, "Get up and go to Zarephath. I have commanded a widow who lives there to feed you."

So Elijah got up and went to Zarephath. As he came into the village, he met a widow gathering firewood. He said to the widow, "Bring me a little water and some bread."

She went to give him some water, but told him, "I have no bread to give you. All I have is a handful of flour and a little oil. I am now gathering a few sticks so that I can cook one last meal for me and my son."

Elijah said, "Don't be afraid. Go ahead and cook your food. But first make me a bit of bread and bring it back here. Then make something for you and your son. This is God's message to you: your jar of flour will not run out and your bottle of oil will not become empty until God sends rain on the land."

The woman did as Elijah told her to. She had enough food for herself and her household. God had provided for her, just as Elijah had said.

Wonder: Imagine being Elijah and trusting that God would provide food and water. Imagine being the woman, wondering how to feed herself and her son.

103

Explore

In this story a prophet spoke up to the king. Think of ways that people today could speak up to their leaders. Are there people in our world today who have had their land taken away wrongly?

Bishop Desmond Tutu from South Africa

Connect

King Ahab realized he had done wrong, and put on sackcloth. How do you show others that you are sorry for what you have done? How do you show God that you are sorry?

Elijah and Naboth's vineyard

1 Kings 21

A man named Naboth had a fine vineyard beside King Ahab's palace in Samaria. The king wanted that vineyard for a vegetable garden, and offered to buy it or give him some other land. Naboth said to Ahab, "No, I will not give up this land. My family has owned it for many, many years."

The king went home angry. He lay down on his bed, turned his face to the wall, and would not eat. Queen Jezebel came to him and asked, "Why are you so upset?" When Ahab told her, she said, "Aren't you the king? You should have whatever you want. Get up and eat some food. Cheer up. I will get Naboth's vineyard for you."

So the queen wrote some letters, pretending they were from Ahab. She ordered people to come together for a special gathering. Naboth would sit at the head of a table and two good-for-nothing men would sit across from him. Then the two men were to tell a lie about Naboth, so that the people would punish him.

And that is what happened. The two men sat across from Naboth and said, "We heard Naboth curse God and the king." Then the people took Naboth outside the city and stoned him to death.

When Jezebel heard that Naboth was dead, she told Ahab to go claim Naboth's vineyard. Ahab went right away. But God told Elijah to meet Ahab at the vineyard. When Ahab saw Elijah he said, "My enemy, have you found me?"

Elijah answered, "Yes, I have found you. You sold yourself to do what is evil in God's sight. Now you will come to ruin because of your evil ways." King Ahab listened to Elijah. He put on sackcloth to show he was sorry.

Wonder: Imagine Naboth standing up to the king to protect his family's land.

Explore
Read the story of Abraham and Sarah on page 27.
What is similar to the story of Elisha and the
Shunammite woman? What is different?

Connect

Death is a painful goodbye. Wouldn't it be wonderful if all the people we love would be healed? We can remember our loved ones who have died and imagine them with God having healthy, healed bodies.

Elisha and the Shunammite woman

2 Kings 4:8–37

Elisha was the son of Shaphat, a farmer. God spoke to the prophet Elijah, telling him that Elisha also would become a prophet. So Elijah looked for Elisha and found him plowing a field. Elisha left his fields, said goodbye to his parents, and followed Elijah. As God had said, Elisha became a prophet himself.

One day, Elisha passed through a town called Shunem. A woman who lived there gave him food to eat. She said to her husband, "I am sure this is a holy man of God. Let's make a room for him so that he can stay with us whenever he is in Shunem."

Elisha was grateful for their kindness and wanted to give them something in return. He learned that the woman wanted a son. Elisha told the woman, "By this time next year you will have a baby boy."

The woman did not believe Elisha, but his promise came true. She gave birth to a baby boy, and she and her husband were very happy.

The boy grew older. But one morning, when he was out with his father in the fields, he complained that his head hurt. Someone carried the boy to his mother. She held him on her lap until noon; then he died. His mother laid him down in Elisha's room. Then she went out and said, "Send me a servant and a donkey. I am going to find Elisha, the holy man of God."

When Elisha learned what had happened, he told his servant to go to the woman's house and lay his staff on the boy's face. But that was not enough for the woman. She said, "I will not leave without you, Elisha."

So Elisha followed the woman back to her house. He went to the room where the boy was lying, and prayed to God. He touched the boy. The boy sneezed seven times and opened his eyes! Elisha sent for the woman and said to her, "Take your son." The woman fell at Elisha's feet and bowed to the ground. Then she took her son and left.

Wonder: Imagine how happy the parents were when their son was born, and how sad they were when he died.

Explore

A slave girl made a difference in Naaman's life. Look for stories of other children changing the world today. What strengths do you have that could make a difference?

108

Connect
What would you do if you were healed from a sickness? How would you thank God?

A young girl and Naaman

2 Kings 5:1–19

Naaman was a mighty commander of the Aramean army and a favorite of the king. But Naaman had a problem: he had a skin disease called leprosy.

On a raid into Israel, the army had captured an Israelite girl. She had become the slave of Naaman's wife. One day the girl said to Naaman's wife, "If only the lord Naaman would go to the prophet in Samaria! He would cure him of his leprosy." Mighty Naaman listened to this young slave girl and went to Israel.

Naaman brought many gifts when he went to Israel. Naaman came to Elisha's house with chariots and horses. Elisha sent a messenger to talk to Naaman. He told Naaman, "Go wash in the Jordan River seven times and you will be healed."

Naaman was furious. He said, "I thought that for me he would come out, call on his god, and heal me. We have better rivers at home than all of the rivers in Israel. Couldn't I wash in them and be healed?"

Naaman started to leave. But his servants said, "Sir, if the prophet had asked you to do something difficult, wouldn't you have done it? So why not do this simple thing?"

So Naaman listened to his servants. He washed himself seven times in the Jordan River. His skin became soft and smooth like the skin of a young child, and he was completely healed. He went back to Elisha. He said, "Now I know your God is the only God. From now on, I will worship God."

Elisha said to Naaman, "Go in peace."

Wonder: I wonder why powerful Naaman listened to advice from the slave girl and his servants.

Elisha turns back the soldiers

2 Kings 6:8–23

Connect

Make a snack or meal for someone you don't see as a friend.

The mighty country of Aram was at war with Israel. The king of Aram called in his officers and said, "We will set up camp over there. When the Israelites come this way, we will capture them."

Elisha the prophet warned the king of Israel, "Your army should beware. The soldiers of Aram are waiting. Take care not to pass that place."

The king of Aram found out that his plans had been ruined. He was furious. "Who told the king of Israel?" the king demanded. "Who is the spy?"

An officer answered, "None of us, my King. It was Elisha, the prophet of God. He tells his king everything, even what you whisper in private." "Then let's capture him," the king decided. "Find out where he is staying."

The Arameans found out that Elisha was staying in Dothan. That night the Aramean soldiers went with horses and chariots and surrounded the city. Early in the morning Elisha's servant saw the soldiers waiting outside and said, "Master! What shall we do?" Elisha replied, "Don't be afraid. God is with us."

Elisha prayed to God, "Strike these people, please, with blindness." God blinded the Aramean soldiers, as Elisha had asked. Then Elisha went to the Arameans and said, "Follow me; I will bring you to the man you are looking for." Elisha led the army into Samaria, straight to the king of Israel. Then God removed their blindness, and they saw they were surrounded by the Israelites.

The king asked, "Elisha, what shall I do now? Shall I kill these soldiers?" "No!" said Elisha. "Prepare a great feast for them. After they eat, send them back to their king."

So the king made a huge feast. Everyone ate and drank. Then they returned home. After that, the armies of Aram did not come raiding into the Israel anymore.

Wonder: The king of Israel asked Elisha for advice. What might have happened if Elisha had told the king to kill the Arameans?

Explore

Talk about ways that you can surprise your friends when you are having a fight. Could you break into song? Dance? Start playing a different game? Do the unusual to help make peace!

111

King Josiah follows God

2 Kings 22:1–23:30

Explore

There is another story of a young king named Joash. You can read his story in the Bible in 2 Chronicles 22–24.

Josiah became king of Judah when he was only eight years old. He faithfully followed God's ways. When Josiah was twenty-six years old, Josiah hired carpenters and builders and stonemasons to repair the temple in Jerusalem.

One day, the high priest Hilkiah had a very surprising message for the king. Hilkiah said, "I have found a book of God's laws in the temple." Josiah's secretary Shaphan brought the scroll to the king and read it to him.

The book had been lost for a very long time, and no one was following these laws of God. No one even remembered these laws. Josiah was so upset that he tore his clothes and cried out loud. He sent a group of his people to ask the prophetess Huldah what God would do.

Huldah answered, "This is what God says: the people should not have forgotten me. They should not have worshiped other gods. But God knows Josiah is truly sorry and God will forgive him."

King Josiah called all the people together and showed them the scroll. He read the law to them. He stood before the people and promised God with all his heart and soul that he would follow all of God's commandments. The people made the same promise.

Then Josiah ordered the people to destroy all of the idols and all of the places where idols had been worshiped.

When the time came to celebrate Passover, King Josiah said, "We must keep the Passover the way the scroll says." All the people celebrated the Passover and they followed the words that were written in the scroll Hilkiah had found.

King Josiah was a good king, and there was no other king like him. He turned to God with all his heart, with all his soul, and with all his might. He helped the people turn to God with all their hearts, as well.

Wonder: Imagine being eight years old and becoming a king or queen!

Connect

Josiah took the words in the scroll seriously, and the people of the land changed their behavior. What words in the Bible do you take seriously? How does this make you change your behavior?

13

114

Connect

Pray for refugees and people who have had to leave their homelands due to war.

Fall of Jerusalem

2 Kings 24:18–25:21

Zedekiah became the king of Judah when he was twenty-one years old. Like some other kings before him, Zedekiah did not follow God's ways. Instead he did things that were evil in God's sight.

At this time, Judah had been conquered by a nation called Babylon. King Zedekiah had to take orders from the Babylonian king, Nebuchadnezzar. Zedekiah did not like this and so he rebelled against Babylon.

King Nebuchadnezzar came with all his soldiers and surrounded the city of Jerusalem. For nearly two years the people could not go in or out of the city. There was no food left for the people and they were starving. King Zedekiah decided to try to escape. He made a hole in the wall of the city and ran away in the night with his army.

But Zedekiah did not get away. The Babylonian soldiers chased after him. His soldiers ran away and the Babylonians caught him and made him a prisoner.

Then the Babylonians broke down the walls of Jerusalem. They destroyed the temple and took away all the valuable things made of bronze, silver, and gold. They burned the houses.

The soldiers carried most of the people off to Babylon. They left only a few of the very poorest people behind to take care of the vineyards.

It was a very sad time and a hard time for the people of Judah.

Wonder: What would it have been like for the people who were carried off to Babylon? What would it have been like to be left behind in a ruined city to care for the vineyards?

Returning to Jerusalem

Ezra 1

The people of Israel lived in Babylon for seventy years. Some of the older people remembered living in Jerusalem. Others had been born in Babylon, not Jerusalem, but they knew that their families had come from another land.

Then, an amazing thing happened. Powerful Babylon was defeated by Persia, so that King Cyrus now ruled the land. And God stirred up Cyrus's spirit, so that the king sent a message through his whole kingdom. The message said, "God has asked me to build a new temple in Jerusalem. Any of you who serve God may return to Jerusalem and rebuild God's house. Your neighbors who remain here will help you by giving you silver, gold, animals, and offerings for the new temple."

Some people were stirred by God's spirit to leave Babylon. Families, priests, and leaders got ready to make the long journey back to Jerusalem. Their neighbors helped them by giving them valuable gifts: household goods, animals, silver, and gold.

King Cyrus himself brought out the treasures that had been stolen from the temple in Jerusalem. He said to Mithredath the treasurer: "Count these treasures and give them back to Sheshbazzar, the prince of Judah."

This was the count: thirty gold basins, one thousand silver basins, twenty-nine knives, thirty gold bowls, four hundred ten silver bowls, and one thousand other containers. Altogether there were 5,400 gold and silver items.

All these things were given to Sheshbazzar to take back to Jerusalem. The people of Israel were ready to go home!

Wonder: Imagine the children who had been born in Babylon. How would they feel about going to a home in Jerusalem that they did not know?

Explore

It was a big decision for King Cyrus of Persia (shown at left) to let the Israelites return to Jerusalem. Look at a Bible map to see how far it would have been to travel by foot from Babylon to Jerusalem.

Rebuilding the temple

Ezra 4–6

Connect

When have you been part of a big project with lots of people working together? What was good or not so good about that experience?

The Jews who made the long journey from Babylon were happy to be back in Jerusalem. They began the big job of rebuilding God's temple.

Some people who lived nearby came to the leaders of the people and said, "We worship God, too. Let us build with you." But the leader Zerubbabel said, "No. You cannot help us build. We will do this job alone, as King Cyrus of Persia commanded us."

This made the people of the land angry. So, instead of helping, they tried to stop the rebuilding progress. They sent a letter to the new king of Persia. They warned that if Jerusalem finished building its walls and temple, the city would refuse to pay taxes to the king.

The king's officials looked through their records. What they found made the king say: "I have discovered that Jerusalem has rebelled against kings in the past. Therefore, I command the people to stop rebuilding the city and the temple."

The work on the temple stopped. But ten years later, prophets spoke to the Jews in Judah and in Jerusalem. They said that Zerubbabel and the others should start their work again.

Now Darius came to the throne of Persia. King Darius found the old decree from King Cyrus, the one that said the people could return to Jerusalem and rebuild the temple. So King Darius gave them permission. He said to the people of the land, "Keep away. Let the people of Israel rebuild their temple. Do not try to stop them." He even said that his royal treasury would pay for the costs.

The people of Israel worked together to finish building the temple. When they finished, they celebrated and made offerings to God.

The time of Passover came. This time the people who had returned from Babylon were joined by some others who lived near them. They all celebrated for seven days, for God had made them joyful. God had caused the king to help them rebuild the temple.

Wonder: The Jews who returned from Babylon wouldn't accept help from the people of the land. Why would they reject help?

Explore

The dates in BCE (Before the Common Era) run backwards in time. The higher the number, the longer ago it was. Find the events of today's story on the timeline.

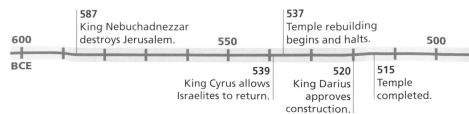

600 BCE

587
King Nebuchadnezzar destroys Jerusalem.

550

539
King Cyrus allows Israelites to return.

537
Temple rebuilding begins and halts.

520
King Darius approves construction.

515
Temple completed.

500

Explore

Read about the Festival of Booths on page 56. In Jerusalem, there were many gates including the Water Gate, the Valley Gate, and the Fish Gate. At nighttime, the city's gates were closed to secure the city.

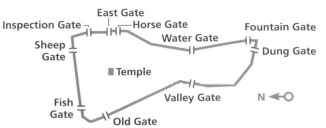

Reading God's word together
Nehemiah 8

All the people gathered together in the square in front of the Water Gate. They asked Ezra the priest to bring the scroll of the Law of Moses, which God had given to Israel.

Ezra stood high on a wooden platform. When he opened the scroll everyone stood up. Ezra blessed the Lord, the great God. All the people lifted their hands and replied, "Amen, Amen." Then they bowed their faces to the ground and worshiped God.

Ezra read the scroll from early morning until midday. Men, women, and everyone who could understand listened to God's word. As Ezra read, the Levites explained the law, so all the people could understand. When the people heard the words, they wept.

Nehemiah the governor and Ezra the priest said to all the people, "Do not be sad and do not cry. Today is God's holy day. Go to your homes and celebrate! Feast on delicious foods. Share your food with people who do not have any. You are strong because you are people of God."

So the people went home, celebrating because they had heard God's word and understood it.

The next day, the leaders of the people, the priests, and the Levites came together with Ezra to study the words of the law. They found that it was time for a festival called the Festival of Booths. Just as it said in the law, the people went out to collect tree branches. They built booths on the roofs and in the courtyards of their houses, in the courts of the temple, and in the city squares.

The people lived in their booths for seven days. This was the first time God's people had celebrated the Festival of Booths for many, many years. For a whole week the people listened to Ezra read from God's word. It was a time of great joy and celebration.

Wonder: I wonder why the people cried when they heard the scroll read aloud.

Explore

The story of Esther is told each year at a Jewish festival called Purim. Whenever Haman's name is mentioned, people in the congregation yell, "Boooo!" Try this as you read the story together.

King Ahasuerus of Persia was also known as Xerxes 1.

Connect
Maybe God has put YOU here for such a time as this! What gifts can you use in the world around you?

Queen Esther

Esther 2–7; 9:24–32

Esther was a young Jewish woman living in Persia. When her parents died, her uncle Mordecai adopted her as his own daughter.

One day, King Ahasuerus sent his servants to find the most beautiful woman in the land to be his queen. Many young women were brought to the palace, and Esther was one of them. Before she left for the palace, Mordecai made her promise not to tell anyone she was a Jew.

When she arrived at the palace, the king loved Esther and made her his queen.

Then the king put Haman in charge of his other officials. He ordered all of his servants to bow down to Haman. Everyone did this—except Mordecai. Mordecai told the king's servants, "I am not a Persian. I am a Jew. That is why I don't bow down to Haman."

Haman was furious and wanted revenge. He decided to try to kill all the Jews in the Persian Empire. "The Jews do not obey your laws," Haman lied to the king. "You should destroy them all." The king agreed.

When Mordecai heard this, he tore his clothes and cried aloud. He told Queen Esther to beg the king to spare their people. Mordecai said, "Perhaps God has made you queen for such a time as this."

Esther knew that anyone who approached the king without his permission could be killed. "I will go to the king," she said, "even though I may die." But the king was not angry. He told Esther he would give her anything she wanted, even half of his kingdom.

Esther said, "I would like to invite you and Haman to come to a special dinner." The king came to Esther's special dinner. He offered again to give her anything she wanted. "I want you to save my people from their enemy," she told the king. "That is my only wish."

"Who is this enemy?" the king demanded, and Esther pointed to Haman.

Then King Ahasuerus declared that all the Jews should be spared. With the help of God, Queen Esther had saved her people.

Wonder: Think about how brave Esther was to come before the king and beg him to spare her people.

123

Explore

Many people wonder why God allows people to suffer. How is God with us even in our suffering and loss?

No one is sure where the land of Uz was located. Theories range from Israel, Jordan, Syrla, Arabia, to Uzbekistan.

Job suffers

The book of Job

There was once a man in the land of Uz named Job. Job loved God and turned away from evil. Job had ten children, thousands of animals, and many servants.

One day, a servant came to Job. "Your oxen and donkeys have been captured and the servants tending them were killed." While he was still speaking, another servant came. "Fire fell from the sky and burned up your sheep and the servants tending them."

Then another servant arrived. "Some raiders stole your camels and killed the servants tending them."

And still another servant told him, "Your sons and daughters were killed when a great wind blew the house down on them."

Job tore his robe. He shaved his head. He cried out, "The Lord gave and the Lord has taken away. Blessed be the name of the Lord."

Job remained faithful to God even when everything went wrong. But one day Job became sick with sores all over his body. He sat in the ashes, scratching his itchy skin with a piece of broken pottery. Job's wife said, "Just give up. It's hopeless."

Job said, "God gives us both good and bad in our lives."

Job's friends came. They wept, tore their clothes, and put dust on their heads. They sat in silence with Job for seven days and seven nights. Later they said that it must be Job's fault and that God must be punishing him.

Job did not blame God, but he was very sad. He said, "I wish I had never been born. I wish that day could be erased from history."

Job wondered why bad things happened when he had tried to follow God's way. Then God answered Job out of a whirlwind. God reminded Job of many things in creation.

In the end, God blessed Job with twice as much as he had before. Job owned thousands of sheep, camels, oxen, and donkeys. He had seven sons and three daughters. Job lived to be an old man and even lived to see his great-grandchildren.

Wonder: Imagine losing everything, like Job did.

God answers Job

Job 38:1–42:6

Explore
In Bible times stormy winds were often seen as a sign from God. Find out which direction a cyclone rotates in the Middle East.

When many terrible things happened to God's servant Job, Job turned to God with a lot of questions. He wondered why all these bad things had happened to him.

Suddenly, from a whirlwind, God answered Job with even more questions to remind Job of the greatness of creation.

"Where were you when I laid the foundations of the earth? Who laid its cornerstone when all the morning stars sang together and the heavenly beings shouted for joy? Have you commanded the morning and caused the dawn to know its place?

"Did you see me lay the boundaries of the seas? Where does light live? Can you show darkness the way home?

"Who tells the clouds to pour out water, and sees that even the desert can produce grass?

"Have you entered the storehouses of the snow? Who has given birth to the frost of heaven? Does lightning listen to you? Who has the wisdom to number the clouds?

"Can you hunt prey for the lions? Who provides food for the raven? Do you know when the mountain goats give birth? Who has let the wild donkey go free? Do you give the horse its strength? Is it by your wisdom that the hawk soars or that the eagle mounts up and makes its nest on high? Speak! Anyone who argues with God must answer."

Job said, "There is nothing I can say. I cannot answer your questions."

God spoke to Job from the whirlwind: "Can you thunder with a voice like mine? Do you wear glory and splendor as I do?

"Look at the behemoth, a large creature that I made. Only I can approach it. Can you catch a large animal with a fishhook? Will you put it on a leash? Who can confront it and stay safe?"

Job thought about all that God could do and said, "I know that you can do all things. I have talked about things that I don't understand. I had heard of you, but now my eye sees you."

Wonder: I wonder why God asked Job so many questions. I wonder if anyone knows the answers.

Connect

Many things in nature can remind us of God's creative power. Take a walk outside to notice small things. Even the smallest insect is a careful creation. The largest oak tree starts as a tiny seed.

127

Explore

This psalm has comforted many people over the years. Try to memorize Psalm 23 so that you know it by heart.

Connect
When have you felt afraid, like you're in a dark valley? When have you felt God by your side, protecting you?

The Lord is my shepherd

Psalm 23

You, Lord, are my shepherd.
You give me everything I need.

You let me rest in green, grassy fields.
You lead me to streams of peaceful water.
You make my soul new again.

You lead me along the right paths.
Even when I walk through dark valleys, I will not be
    afraid.
You are with me, and your staff protects me.

You make a feast for me in front of those who are against
    me.
You fill my cup until it overflows.

Your kindness and love will be with me every day of my
    life,
And I will live in your house forever.

Wonder: Imagine that you are a sheep, able to trust the shepherd for everything that you need.

129

Explore

Go for a walk and talk about the great variety in creation, from plants and trees to planets in the universe. Notice animal homes.

130

Connect

Write your own psalm of praise for the things you love in creation.

God cares for the earth

Psalm 104

Bless the Lord, O my soul.
God, you are very great.
Light wraps around you like clothing.
You ride on the wind with the clouds as your chariot.

You gave the earth a strong foundation,
and covered it with water, even above the mountains.
Then you made the waters run down into the valleys.

You make springs of water in the valleys
so that every bird and animal has water.
You make the grass grow for the cattle,
and plants for people to use.
You bring good food from the earth.

The trees provide homes for the birds.
The high mountains are home to wild goats.
The rocks give shelter to wild rabbits.

The moon marks the seasons.
The sun knows what time to set.
You make darkness and night.

God, you have made so many things.
In wisdom you have made them all.
The earth is full of your creatures.

Yonder is the great wide sea.
Creeping things, too many to count, live there;
living things both great and small.

All the creatures look to you for food.
When you open your hand,
the animals are filled with good things.
New life comes from you, God.
Your spirit renews the land.

May God rejoice in all creation.
I will sing to God as long as I live.
Bless the Lord, O my soul. Praise God!

Wonder: This psalm uses poetic language to talk about many wonderful things in God's world. What part of the psalm do you like best?

Trust in God's care

Psalm 121

Explore

This psalm is called a "song of ascent." This may be because people sang this psalm as they traveled to worship in Jerusalem. Look at a relief map of Israel to see the many hills.

I lift up my eyes to the hills—
from where will my help come?
My help comes from the Lord,
who made heaven and earth.

God will not let your foot slip;
God who keeps you will not slumber.
The one who keeps Israel
will neither slumber nor sleep.

God is the one who guards and protects you.
God is the shade at your right hand.
The hot sun shall not harm you by day.
You will be safe in the moonlit night.

God will keep you from evil.
God will be with you as you go out and come in,
now and always.

Wonder: How does God watch over you and help you?
Imagine journeying far from home and hearing this prayer
at bedtime.

Connect

Have you ever stood under a starlit sky and wondered about God? This psalm would be fun to read as you travel or go camping.

Prayer of Agur

Proverbs 30:7–9

Connect
Pray the Lord's Prayer together with others. Especially notice the line "Give us this day our daily bread." What are the things that you need to live well? What things could you do without?

Agur son of Jakeh prayed these words:

O God, I ask you for two things. Please give them to me as long as I live.

> Keep lying and falseness far away from me.
> Do not give me poverty or wealth, but feed me with the food I need.

If I am wealthy, I might forget about you, God.
If I am so poor that I have nothing to eat, I might need to steal food or be tempted to speak against God.

> O God, give me just enough but not too much.
> Feed me with the food I need.

Wonder: I wonder how Agur decided which two things to ask for.

Explore

Proverbs are short sayings or tiny recipes for living wisely. Read Proverbs 6:30–31; 14:31; 22:2–9. Why might people steal? Is it better to be rich or poor? Which proverb do you want to remember?

Explore

Find out about people turning weapons into useful tools. Some turn nuclear weapon material into jewelry, some turn swords into gardening tools, some turn guns into beautiful artwork. See if you can find an example online.

Guns into Plowshares
by Esther Augsburger

Connect
Imagine a world without war or fighting.
Imagine plenty of food growing in fields and
gardens.

Walk in the light of the Lord

Isaiah 2:1–5

The prophet Isaiah brought a message to God's people.

In days to come, the house of God will be raised above
   every hill.
People from every part of the earth will come to worship
   God and to learn about God's ways.

Everyone will walk in God's paths of peace and love.
A new time will come when wars will end.
God's ways will bring peace instead of fighting.

God shall judge between the nations,
and shall arbitrate for many peoples;
they shall beat their swords into plowshares,
and their spears into pruning hooks;
nation shall not lift up sword against nation,
neither shall they learn war any more.

Come, let us walk in God's light. Come, let us live in the
   light of God.

Wonder: I wonder how people can walk God's path. I
wonder why people turn weapons into tools.

Comfort for God's people

Isaiah 40

Connect
How can you show comfort to someone who is going through hard times? What comforts you when you are upset?

The prophet Isaiah brought words of hope to the people of Israel:

Comfort, O comfort my people, says your God.
Speak tenderly to Jerusalem. Cry out, "Your punishment is finished."

Make a straight highway in the desert for our God.
Every valley shall be lifted up, and every mountain made low.
People are like grass that withers,
But God's word will stand forever.

The Lord God comes with strength.
God feeds the flock like a shepherd, gathering the lambs,
And gently carrying them to the mother sheep.

Who else can measure the waters or weigh the mountains?
Is there anyone who taught God or showed God the path of justice?
To God, all the nations in the world are like a drop of water.

Is there anyone like God?
God asks, "Who is equal to me? Who created the stars?"
God numbers them and calls them all by name.

Do you not know? Have you not heard?
The Lord is the everlasting God, the Creator of the ends of the earth.
God never gets tired.
God understands more than we could ever know.
God gives strength to the powerless.
Even young people will get tired and fall down exhausted.

But those who wait for the Lord shall renew their strength;
they shall mount up with wings like eagles;
they shall run and not be weary, they shall walk and not faint.

Wonder: I wonder how Isaiah knew God was coming to help and comfort.

Explore

Perhaps Isaiah's message came when the Israelites were sent into exile. They needed comfort and strength at that time. Look for information about the strong short-toed eagle that lives in Bible lands.

Peace for all

Isaiah 65:17–25

Connect
The prophet Isaiah dreamed of a time when everyone would have enough, and where people and animals would live peacefully with each other. What are your dreams for the world?

Isaiah saw a vision of peace and heard God's voice say:

"I am creating a new heaven and earth. Be glad and celebrate what I am doing for my people.

"A time will come when there will be no more sadness or crying. Babies will be healthy and grownups will live long, good lives.

"Everyone will have a house of their own to live in. People will plant gardens and have enough food. Everyone will have what they need. God will bless them.

"I will answer before anyone needs to call.
I will hear even before they have finished speaking.

"All creatures will live together in peace.
The wolf and the lamb will eat together.
The lion will eat straw like the ox.

"On my holy mountain, no one will ever hurt or destroy another."

This is the vision of peace that Isaiah shared with the people.

Wonder: Imagine prey and predator animals sharing food.

Explore

Compare this to the vision of a new heaven and new earth in Revelation 21 on page 314. What is similar? What is different?

The Peaceable Kingdom by Edward Hicks

Jeremiah and a new covenant

Jeremiah 1:1–10; 31:31–40

Connect

God calls people of all ages. How old are you? What big thing could you do with God's help?

Jeremiah, the son of the priest Hilkiah, lived in Anathoth, in the land of Benjamin. When he was still a boy, he heard the voice of God speaking to him: "Before you were even born, I knew you and chose you to be a prophet."

Jeremiah said, "But, God, I am too young. I don't know how to speak to people."

God answered, "Do not say that you are too young. You will go where I send you and you will speak the messages I give you. Do not be afraid. I will be with you."

Then God touched Jeremiah's mouth and said, "I have put my words in your mouth. I am calling you to speak to nations. Sometimes your words will help pull down what needs to be destroyed. Sometimes your words will cause seeds of new life to grow."

God first spoke to Jeremiah when Josiah was king of Judah. Many years later, when Jeremiah was much older, Jerusalem was captured and many of its people were taken to Babylon. In the midst of these hard times, Jeremiah brought a message of hope.

Jeremiah spoke for God: "The time is coming when I will make a new covenant with Israel and Judah. It will not be like the old covenant. The people broke that covenant even though I led them out of slavery in Egypt.

"This is the covenant that I will make: I will put my law within the people, and I will write it on their hearts. I will be their God, and they shall be my people. I will forgive the wrong they have done; and they shall all know me, from the least important to the most powerful."

Jeremiah continued, "This is what God says: 'As long as the sun, the stars, and the moon stay in their places and the waves of the seas continue to roll, the people of Israel will be my people.

'The time is coming when the walls of the city will be rebuilt. The valley and all that surrounds the city will be sacred places, and this will be true forever.'"

Wonder: Imagine Jeremiah being young then growing old. Was it hard or easy to bring God's message to the people?

Explore

Jeremiah said God's will for the people would be in their hearts or in their understanding. Read Exodus 20:2, at the beginning of the Ten Commandments. What is a good reason for following God's law?

The path to God's promise

Jeremiah 33:14–16; Psalm 25

Connect

People long ago went through hard times just as we do today. Who helps you when you are lonely and sad?

The prophet Jeremiah brought this message from God:

"The time is coming when I will keep my promise
to the people of Israel and Judah.
A ruler will spring up like a branch on a tree.
A leader will come who will set things right.
In those days, the people of Jerusalem will be safe.
The people will say, 'God shows us what is right.'"

The people of long ago also sang a psalm about God's
     promise:

I lift my soul to you, O God.
O my God, I trust in you.

Do not let anyone insult me.
Do not let my enemies laugh at me.

Make me know your ways, O God.
Teach me your paths of truth.
I wait for you all day long.

God, remember the love you have shown your people.
Out of your goodness, do not remember my sins.
Forgive me when I do wrong.

All the paths of the Lord are steadfast love.
The friendship of the Lord is for those who follow.

Turn to me, O God, and be kind to me, for I am lonely
     and sad.
Forgive me for what I've done wrong.

May justice and goodness save me, for I wait for you, O
     God.
Save Israel from of all its troubles.

Wonder: How could a ruler spring up like a branch on a tree?

144

Explore

Go for a walk as a family. Talk about what it means to walk in God's paths.

Ezekiel and the dry bones

Ezekiel 37:1–14

Connect

Is there anything in your school or neighborhood that seems like "dry bones"? Where could God breathe new life?

While the people lived in far-off Babylon, they often thought about their homeland. Prophets like Jeremiah and Ezekiel gave hope to the people.

Ezekiel was a prophet who had a vision, a dream sent from God. In his vision, Ezekiel was in a deserted valley where many people had died. There were many bones in this valley, and they were very dry.

God asked Ezekiel, "Can these bones live?"

"Oh, God, you are the one who knows," answered Ezekiel.

"Speak to the bones," God said. "Say, 'O dry bones, God will cause breath to enter you, and you shall live.'"

So Ezekiel spoke to the dry bones. The bones rattled and came together and were covered with skin. They looked like people without any life in them—they did not breathe.

Then Ezekiel said, "Come from the four winds, O breath. Breathe upon these people, so they may live." Then breath came into the bodies. Life came into the bodies. They stood on their feet, and the valley was suddenly alive with people, too many to count.

God said to Ezekiel, "The bones are like the people of Israel who say, 'Our bones are dried up and our hope is lost. What will happen to us?'"

Ezekiel told his dream to the people and gave them this message: "God says, 'O my people, I will put my spirit within you, and you shall live. I will place you on your own soil; then you shall know that I have spoken and will act.'"

Wonder: How could people feel like dry bones?

Explore

This story fits with the Fall of Jerusalem story on page 114. Try to imagine the people living in exile. Look for pictures of the Ishtar gate or other reconstructions from the Babylonian Empire. The photo at left shows one of the dragons sculpted in the Ishtar gate.

Shadrach, Meshach, and Abednego

Daniel 3

Connect
Sometimes we need to say "no." Can you think of a time when you said "no" to something that you knew was wrong?

King Nebuchadnezzar of Babylon made a huge, golden statue. He called all the officers in the kingdom to come see it. The king's servant told the people: "When you hear the sound of many instruments playing, you must bow down and worship this statue. Anyone who does not will be thrown into a fire!"

The instruments played and all the people—almost all the people—fell down and worshiped the statue. But Shadrach, Meshach, and Abednego did not bow down. These three men were Israelites, but Nebuchadnezzar had given them important jobs in his kingdom.

Some people came to Nebuchadnezzar. They said, "O King, live forever! Do you know that Shadrach, Meshach, and Abednego have ignored your order? They do not serve your gods and they do not worship your golden statue."

King Nebuchadnezzar was angry. He ordered Shadrach, Meshach, and Abednego to come to him. He said, "Is it true what I hear? I will give you another chance. But if you don't bow down to my statue this time, you will be thrown into the fire. Can your god save you from that?"

Shadrach, Meshach, and Abednego answered, "O King, our God may be able to save us. But if not, we still will not worship your statue." This answer made the king so angry that he had his strongest guards throw the three Israelites into the blazing fire.

Then Nebuchadnezzar looked into the fire. To his surprise, he saw not three, but four people in the fire. They were not hurt at all—and the fourth one looked like a god. Nebuchadnezzar called, "Shadrach, Meshach, and Abednego, come out!"

When the three walked out to the king, their hair and clothes were not burnt. They didn't even smell like smoke.

King Nebuchadnezzar cried out, "Blessed be the God of Shadrach, Meshach, and Abednego, who sent an angel to save them. They were willing to die rather than worship another god. So here is the new rule. No one may say anything against their God. There is no other god who can save like this."

Wonder: Why do you think that King Nebuchadnezzar wanted people to bow down to a huge statue?

Explore

Talk about people who have stood up for what they believed. Learn more about people like Oscar Romero, Leymah Gbowee, and Dr. Julieta Castellanos. Light a candle to honor someone's courageous story.

Anneken Hendricks was burned at the stake in Amsterdam, 1571, for her beliefs.

149

Explore

Air is all around us, just like God's presence. Daniel believed that God was with him in the lions' den. Compare the closeness of air to God's presence with us.

150

Connect
What frightens you? Picture God with you
during those times.

Daniel stands up to the king

Daniel 6

Darius, king of Persia, had 120 satraps in his kingdom. They reported to three presidents. Daniel, a Jew, was one of these presidents. Daniel was very good at his job, and King Darius planned to put him in charge of the whole kingdom.

The other presidents and satraps were jealous. They wanted to get Daniel in trouble with the king, but Daniel had done nothing wrong. So they came up with a plan.

"O King Darius," they said, "may you live forever! You should make a law that whoever prays to anyone but you must be fed to the lions. Sign this law, O King, so that it can never be changed."

The king signed the law. Daniel knew about the law, but he still went home, opened the windows, got down on his knees, and prayed to God. He prayed three times every day, just as he always had.

The satraps and presidents came and found Daniel praying. "O King," they said, "didn't you sign a law that said people could only pray to you? And that if they prayed to anyone else, they would be fed to the lions?"

King Darius agreed. The satraps and presidents continued, "Daniel is ignoring you and your law. He still prays to his God three times a day!"

The king was horrified. All day long he tried to find a way to save Daniel. But he could not change the law that he had signed. So Daniel was thrown into the den of lions. The king said to him, "May your God save you." Then a stone sealed the mouth of the lions' den.

That night, the king could not eat or sleep. At daybreak he hurried to the lions' den. "Daniel," he called, "has your God saved you?" Daniel answered, "O King, live forever! God sent an angel to shut the mouths of the lions."

When Daniel was brought out, unharmed, from the lions' den, the king commanded, "All people should worship the God of Daniel. This is the living God, enduring forever!"

Wonder: Why do you suppose Daniel didn't hide when he prayed?

The prophets call for justice

Amos 5:14–24; Micah 6:1–8

Connect
Discuss an unfair situation your family knows about. How could you help? Who will you be kind to today?

Amos and Micah were two of the prophets who reminded people how to follow God.

Amos was a shepherd. He tended his sheep but also heard messages from God. Amos told the people: "Do good, and you will live. God will be with you. Work for justice in the city. If you don't, there will be sadness everywhere."

Amos spoke for God, saying, "Doing good is more important than worship and sacrifices. Are you being fair to your neighbors? Are you feeding the poor people in your city? Real worship is doing good to others."

Amos went on, "If you do all these things, God will be with you. Justice will roll down like a waterfall. Goodness will be like a stream that flows forever."

Micah also spoke to the people. He said, "Listen to what God says!"

God says, "Tell the mountains and the hills! I have a problem with Israel."

"I am not pleased. Don't you remember how you were suffering in Egypt so long ago? Don't you remember how I sent Moses, Aaron, and Miriam to help you? I brought you out of the land of Egypt, out of the house of slavery. I saved you many, many times!"

The people said, "How should we worship God? Should we give burnt offerings? Will God be pleased with thousands of rams? With ten thousand rivers of oil? Will that make God happy?"

The prophet Micah spoke: "God has told you, oh people, what is good. This is what God wants from you: do justice, love kindness, and walk humbly with your God. That is God's way."

Wonder: I wonder what the people of Israel thought when they heard these messages from the prophets.

Great Sea

ISRAEL

Samaria

Jerusalem

Moresheth Tekoa

JUDAH

Jordan River

Dead Sea

Israel and Judah
for Amos
and Micah

Explore
Amos, a farmer from Tekoa, and Micah, from the small town of Moresheth, brought God's message to people long ago. Their messages still speak to us today. Look up the Bible references for this story and choose one verse to memorize.

The story of Jonah

The book of Jonah

Connect

Jonah went in the opposite direction that God told him to. When have you done exactly the opposite of what you were supposed to do?

God told the prophet Jonah, "Go to Nineveh and tell the people that they are doing wrong." But instead, Jonah boarded a boat sailing to Tarshish, went below, and fell asleep.

Then a big storm came up. The captain said to Jonah, "Get up! Pray. Maybe your god will save us!"

The storm did not stop. The sailors were terrified. Jonah said, "Throw me into the sea. This storm is because of me." The sailors did not want to, but finally, they picked Jonah up and threw him into the sea. The storm stopped.

God sent a large fish to swallow Jonah. Jonah was in its belly for three days and nights. There he prayed to God. "Thank you, God, for hearing me! I will keep my promise to you." Then God told the fish to spit Jonah onto land.

God told Jonah again, "Go to Nineveh." This time Jonah went. He walked across Ninevah, crying out God's message, "Forty more days, and Nineveh will be destroyed!"

When the king of Nineveh heard the news, he put on sackcloth. He sat in ashes and proclaimed, "No one shall eat or drink anything. Everyone must wear sackcloth and cry out to God. We must turn away from evil and violence. May God forgive us."

God saw this and did not destroy the city. This made Jonah angry. He said, "God, I knew this would happen. That's why I did not want to come here. I know that you are gracious, loving, and forgiving! I cannot bear it."

Jonah went out of the city. He sat there, waiting to see what would happen next. God made a bush grow up to give Jonah shade. Jonah was happy about the bush. But the next day, a worm attacked the bush and it died. The sun beat down. Jonah said, "I cannot bear this!"

God asked, "Is it right for you to be angry about the bush?" Jonah said, "Yes, angry enough to die."

God said, "You care about the bush. Do you really think that I should not care about Nineveh? That city has many, many people who do not understand right and wrong, and also many animals."

Wonder: Why did Jonah not want God to forgive the people of Nineveh?

Explore

Nineveh was a royal city in the Assyrian empire. God showed Jonah that God's love is so broad that it even encompasses Jonah's worst enemy. Who are the people that you can think of who are inside God's big circle of love?

Connect

Imagine a city near you—full of young children playing and old people visiting on park benches. Draw a picture of that scene.

156

Explore

Zechariah's name means "God remembers." Can you find another Zechariah in the Bible?

Peace in the city

Zechariah 8:1–8

The prophet Zechariah had a vision of the world God wanted to see.

In Zechariah's vision, God said, "The people will come back to Jerusalem and I will live with them. It will be a holy city. Old men and old women will sit on benches and visit. The city will be full of boys and girls, laughing and playing. It may seem impossible to you, but it is possible for me.

"People will come from the eastern countries. People will come from the western countries. I will bring them together in Jerusalem and bless them. They shall be my people and I will be their God. I will be faithful to the people and the people will be faithful to me."

Wonder: What does Zechariah's dream look like for children? For grandparents? For the land?

Zechariah and Elizabeth

Luke 1:5–25, 57–80

Connect

Zechariah was surprised by the angel. Think of a time when you were surprised. How did you respond?

The priest Zechariah and his wife, Elizabeth, were faithful followers of God. They had been married for a long time, but did not have children.

Zechariah took turns with the other priests working in the temple. One day Zechariah was chosen to take the incense inside the holy place. As he did this, the people stood outside the curtain praying.

When Zechariah stepped into the holy place, he saw an angel beside the altar. He was very frightened. But the angel said, "Do not be afraid, Zechariah. Your prayer has been heard. Elizabeth will have a son, and you will name him John. You will be glad, and many will rejoice at his birth. He will be like the prophet Elijah. He will help people follow God."

"How will I know this is so?" Zechariah asked. "My wife and I are both old."

"I am Gabriel," said the angel. "I stand in the presence of God. I have been sent to bring you this message. But since you did not believe my words, you will not be able to speak until the day my words come true."

The people praying outside wondered why it was taking the priest so long. When Zechariah came out, he couldn't talk. The people realized he'd seen a vision.

It happened as the angel said. Elizabeth became pregnant. Throughout the whole nine months of waiting for the baby, Zechariah could not speak.

After the birth, the neighbors gathered to celebrate. "Elizabeth had a baby in her old age!" they said. "He will be named Zechariah just like his father."

"Not Zechariah," said Elizabeth. "His name will be John."

The neighbors were surprised. No one else in the family was named John. They turned to Zechariah and asked him what he wanted the baby to be called. Zechariah wrote on a tablet, "His name is John."

Suddenly, Zechariah could talk again and he said to the people, "Blessed be the name of the Lord. God has remembered us and shown mercy."

Then he said to his son John, "And you, child, will be a prophet. You will prepare the way and help people return to God. God's light will shine upon us and guide us in the way of peace."

Wonder: I wonder how God guides us in the way of peace.

Explore

An angel is a messenger from God. How do you send messages to others? How can you send a message of God's love?

Explore

Read the story of Hannah and her baby Samuel in 1 Samuel 1–2 and on page 83 of this book. How is Hannah's prayer like Mary's? How are these stories similar to and different from each other?

Connect
Mary's prayer proclaimed the great things that God had done. What great things has God done for you? Can you sing a song about them?

Mary says yes

Luke 1:26–56

This story takes place between the beginning and end of the previous story.

Mary lived in Nazareth of Galilee, a small village far from Jerusalem. She was young and engaged to marry Joseph, a carpenter.

One day the angel Gabriel came to her. "Greetings, favored one. God is with you," said the angel.

Mary was confused. What could the angel mean by this?

Gabriel said, "Do not be afraid, Mary. God has chosen you to be the mother of Jesus. He will be great and will be called Son of God."

"How can this be?" asked Mary.

"God's spirit will make it possible. Your relative Elizabeth is pregnant in her old age. Nothing will be impossible with God."

Then Mary said, "Here am I, the servant of God. Let it happen just as you have said." Then the angel left her.

Mary set out to visit Elizabeth in the hill country of Judea. When Mary entered her home, Elizabeth ran to greet her.

"You and your baby are blessed by God," said Elizabeth. "And I am blessed because the mother of my Lord has come to visit me. At the sound of your voice, the baby inside me leaped for joy."

Mary prayed aloud, praising God with all her heart: "My soul magnifies the Lord, and my spirit rejoices in God, my Savior. Although I am lowly, God has done great things for me. Surely, people for years and years to come will call me blessed.

"God shows mercy to the faithful. God has brought down the powerful from their thrones, and lifted up the lowly. God has filled the hungry with good things, and sent the rich away empty. God watches over us, keeping the promise made to our ancestor Abraham."

Mary stayed with Elizabeth for about three months. Then she returned to her home.

Wonder: Why did God choose Mary from all of the other women at that time?

161

An angel visits Joseph

Matthew 1:1–25

Connect
The angel told Joseph of an amazing plan for his life. What extraordinary plans might God have for you?

The stars shone this night just as they had for Joseph's ancestor, Abraham. There had been so many generations since then: Joseph's parents and grandparents and great-grandparents and great-great-grandparents—and on and on, two thousand years of "greats."

There were Isaac, Jacob, Rahab, Boaz, Ruth, and Jesse, the father of King David. Many men and women over many years linked Abraham and King David to Joseph. When Joseph married Mary, Jesus the Messiah would belong to the family of Abraham.

Joseph was engaged to be married to Mary. Then he learned that she was going to have a baby. The law said that he should tell everyone and call off the wedding.

Joseph didn't want people to say awful things about Mary. He didn't want anyone to harm her. Finally, he decided that he would simply end their engagement very quietly. Thinking about this, he fell asleep.

While Joseph slept, an angel came to him in a dream. "Joseph, go ahead and take Mary for your wife," the angel said. "The baby that she will have is from the Holy Spirit. It will be a boy and you are to name him Jesus. He will save the people from their sins."

Joseph awoke. He trusted God and did what God's angel had told him to do. Mary and Joseph were married. When the baby was born, they named him Jesus.

Wonder: I wonder how Joseph felt when he heard that Mary's baby would be so special.

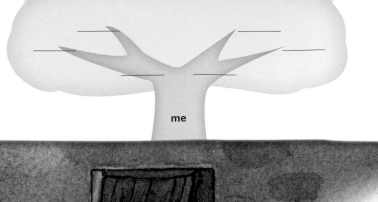

me

Explore

This story talks about Jesus' ancestors, the people from Jesus' family who lived long ago. Sometimes this is called a genealogy or a family tree. Who is in your family tree?

Jesus is born

Luke 2:1–7

Explore

The name Jesus means "God has saved." Sometimes Jesus is also called "Emmanuel," which means "God with us." What is the meaning of your name?

In those days, the emperor Augustus ruled over many lands and many, many people. Emperor Augustus decided that he wanted a list of every person in his realm.

He ordered everyone to go to the towns where their ancestors had come from. This is where they would have to put their names on the emperor's list.

This meant that many people had to travel a long way. Joseph, who came from the family of King David, would have to travel from his home in Nazareth in Galilee to the city of Bethlehem in Judea, which was known as the city of David.

Joseph made the long trip to Bethlehem with Mary, who was expecting her first child. While they were in Bethlehem, the time came for Mary to have her baby.

Mary and Joseph could not find room in the inn where travelers usually stayed. They found shelter in a place for animals, and there Mary gave birth to her firstborn son, Jesus.

Mary wrapped her baby in bands of cloth. When it was time for him to sleep, she laid him in a manger, the animals' feeding trough.

Wonder: Imagine a mother having a baby far away from home and in a place where animals are kept.

Connect

Have you ever held a newborn baby? What do you think it felt like for Mary to hold her son Jesus for the first time?

165

Explore

At this time, shepherds were not very important people and they were often poor. Can you think of other Bible stories where God chose people who were poor or small to do important jobs?

166

Connect

The angels praised God saying, "Glory to God and peace on earth." What do you think peace on earth would look like?

Shepherds show the way

Luke 2:8–20

In the fields outside Bethlehem, shepherds were keeping watch over their flocks of sheep. All of a sudden an angel stood before them and God's glory shone around them. The shepherds were terrified.

The angel said, "Do not be afraid! I am bringing you good news of great joy for all people. Today, in the city of David, a Savior is born. This is Christ the Lord. You will find a child wrapped in bands of cloth and lying in a manger." Suddenly there were many, many angels all around, praising God and saying, "Glory to God and peace on earth!"

When the angels left, the shepherds said, "Let's go to Bethlehem and see what has happened." They went quickly and found Mary, Joseph, and the child. They told Mary and Joseph what the angels had said about the baby.

The shepherds then returned to their fields. As they went, they praised God for all they had heard and seen. Everyone who heard the news was amazed.

Mary sat quietly and thought about what the shepherds had told them. She kept their words in her heart, like a treasure.

Wonder: Why were the shepherds the first ones to hear the news of Jesus' birth?

Explore

Anna was a prophet, someone who served God in the temple and who helped others to live in God's way. Look in your Bible and find out about other women prophets like Deborah, Huldah, and Miriam. At right: Deborah sits as judge for Israel.

Connect
How does your church community welcome and bless babies?

Simeon and Anna

Luke 2:21–40

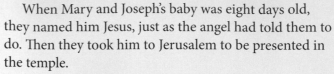

When Mary and Joseph's baby was eight days old, they named him Jesus, just as the angel had told them to do. Then they took him to Jerusalem to be presented in the temple.

An old man named Simeon lived in Jerusalem. God's spirit had told Simeon that he would see the Messiah before he died. Simeon had lived a long time, hoping and waiting for the time when he would see the Messiah.

On the day that baby Jesus was brought to Jerusalem, God's spirit led Simeon to the temple. When he saw Mary and Joseph and the baby, Simeon took Jesus into his arms. He praised God, saying, "Now you are letting your servant go in peace. This child will bring glory to Israel. This child will bring light to the whole world."

Joseph and Mary were amazed. Then Simeon blessed them too. And he said to Mary, "Your son will bring hope to many people. But he will also make some people very angry. This will be like a sword that will pierce your own soul, too."

Then a prophet named Anna came forward. Anna was eighty-four years old. She prayed in the temple at night and during the day.

When Anna saw the baby, she praised God. She talked about the baby Jesus to everyone who would listen.

Then Mary and Joseph returned to their town of Nazareth, in Galilee. They lived there and Jesus continued to grow. He became strong and full of wisdom. He was blessed by God.

Wonder: I wonder what Simeon and Anna noticed about Jesus that made them praise God.

A visit from the magi

Matthew 2:1–12

Connect

The wise men brought Jesus the best gifts they could offer. What are the best gifts that you can offer Jesus?

In the time of King Herod, after Jesus was born, wise men, or magi, from the East came to Jerusalem. They asked, "Where is the child who has been born king of the Jews? We have seen his star in the night sky, and we want to bring him gifts and worship him."

King Herod heard what the magi were saying, and he was frightened. He did not want anyone else claiming to be king in his land. He asked the chief priests and teachers of the law what they knew about this child. They told Herod that the prophets had written that a new king would be born in Bethlehem.

King Herod secretly called for the wise men to come to him. He said, "Go and search for this child. When you find him, let me know so that I may also go and worship him."

When the magi left the king, they followed the star from Jerusalem to Bethlehem. The star stopped over a house. They went in and saw young Jesus with his mother. They knelt before him and worshiped him. They opened their treasure chests and offered him gold, and precious spices of frankincense and myrrh.

That night the magi were warned in a dream not to go back to King Herod. So they returned to their own country by a different road.

Wonder: Imagine what it would be like to take a long journey with only a star to guide you.

King Herod the Great

171

Explore

The cities of Nazareth and Bethlehem and the country of Egypt all still exist. Look at the map and see how far Joseph, Mary, and Jesus had to travel on foot!

Connect

Imagine arriving at a safe place after a long and dangerous journey. What can you do to make newcomers feel safe in your neighborhood?

Escape to Egypt

Matthew 2:13–23

One night, while Joseph was asleep, an angel spoke to him in a dream: "Get up and run away to Egypt with Mary and Jesus. King Herod is sending people to hunt for your child and wants to destroy him."

Joseph got up and woke Mary. In the darkness, they took Jesus and fled.

Joseph, Mary, and the boy Jesus traveled many days until they reached the country of Egypt. When King Herod discovered that he had been tricked by the wise men, he was furious. He sent his soldiers to kill all the young children who lived near Bethlehem. He thought that would get rid of this young king of the Jews.

Joseph, Mary, and Jesus lived in Egypt for a time. When Herod died, an angel again came to Joseph in a dream.

"Joseph," the angel said, "Get up and go to the land of Israel. King Herod is dead and can no longer hurt Jesus."

Joseph, Mary, and Jesus began the long journey across the desert. But in another dream, Joseph learned that Herod's son was now ruling in Judea, so they were afraid to go there.

Instead, the family traveled to Galilee. They made their home in the town of Nazareth and lived safely there.

Wonder: Why would a king act the way Herod did?

Studying at the temple

Luke 2:41–52

Connect

Jesus and the temple leaders were learning about God together. Where do you like to learn about God?

Every year Mary and Joseph traveled to Jerusalem for the Passover festival. The year that Jesus was twelve they went to the festival as usual, along with a group of others from the same region.

When the festival was over, the group came together and began the journey back home. Mary and Joseph did not see Jesus as they walked along on that first day, but they were not worried. There were many friends and family members along, and they were sure he was with some of them.

When evening came, though, they started looking for Jesus. He was nowhere among their friends and relatives. When they could not find him, they turned back to Jerusalem to look there.

After searching in Jerusalem for three days, Mary and Joseph finally found Jesus. He was in the temple with the teachers, listening and asking questions. Everyone who heard him was amazed.

Mary said, "Child, why have you treated us like this? Your father and I have been so worried. We have searched everywhere for you."

Jesus answered, "Why were you looking for me? Didn't you know that I had to be here in my Father's house?" Mary and Joseph didn't understand what Jesus meant.

Jesus went back to Nazareth with his parents and obeyed them. His mother treasured these things in her heart. Jesus grew in body and spirit, blessed both by people and by God.

Wonder: I wonder why Jesus wasn't worried or feeling lost.

A model of the temple in Jerusalem where Jesus was found

Explore

Isaiah and John were both prophets who tried to help God's people to change their ways. What people in your community help others to be more loving? Maybe they're prophets too!

176

Connect
John asked people to change their ways. What unfair things should be changed in our world today?

John the Baptist shows the way

Mark 1:1–8

Many years earlier, the prophet Isaiah had said that someone would come to prepare the way, and that a voice would call out in the wilderness.

A man named John began preaching in the wilderness near the Jordan River. John was the son of Elizabeth and Zechariah. When he grew up, he became known as John the Baptizer, or John the Baptist.

John the Baptist wore strange clothes made from camel's hair, and wore a leather belt around his waist. He ate locusts and wild honey. John said to people, "Get ready. Change your ways. Then you will be forgiven for your sins."

Many people heard about John and his message and came to be baptized by him. They came from the city of Jerusalem. They came from the small towns and villages. They came from all over Judea. John baptized them in the water of the Jordan River.

John told everyone, "There's someone coming who is much more powerful than I am. I am not even good enough to untie his sandals. I have baptized you with water, but he will baptize you with the Holy Spirit."

Wonder: John said, "Someone powerful is coming." I wonder who John was talking about.

Jesus is baptized

Matthew 3:13–17; Mark 1:9–11; Luke 3:21–22; John 1:29–34

Explore
See if you can find photos of the Jordan River and imagine Jesus and John along its banks. What direction does the Jordan River flow?

Many people heard about John the Baptist. They came to the Jordan River to find out what was happening. They heard John preach. They confessed their sins and were baptized by John in the river.

People talked about John's clothes, woven from camel hair. They talked about the desert foods he ate, locusts and wild honey. Most important, they talked about John's words.

John had told them something new was happening. "The one who is more powerful than I am is coming. He will baptize you with the Holy Spirit."

Jesus came to the Jordan to be baptized by John. John said, "You should not be coming to me; I am the one who needs to be baptized by you."

But Jesus said, "No, it is right for you to baptize me now."

So John agreed, and he baptized Jesus in the river.

As Jesus came up out of the water, he saw the heavens open. The Holy Spirit descended like a dove and rested on him, and a voice came from heaven, "You are my Son, the Beloved; with you I am well pleased."

Wonder: I wonder how people felt after they had been baptized by John. How do you think their lives changed?

Connect

Baptism is still practiced in Christian churches. Have you seen a baptism recently? Describe the baptism practices in your congregation.

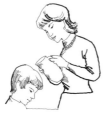

Three methods of baptism (left to right): immersion, pouring, and sprinkling

179

Explore

Devil means "adversary" or being against. It is the opposite of offering support. The devil challenged Jesus to reject God's way, but Jesus stayed true to God's love. Who or what helps you do the right thing?

Connect

Jesus often spent time alone so that he could listen to God in the silence. Create a special place where you can spend a few minutes each day just being quiet with God.

Jesus in the desert

Matthew 4:1–11; Mark 1:12–13; Luke 4:1–13

After Jesus was baptized, God's spirit led him to the wilderness, where he prayed and fasted for forty days.

At the end of that time, he was famished with hunger. Then the devil came to him and said, "If you are the Son of God, command these stones to become loaves of bread."

But Jesus answered, "I will not. It is written, 'One does not live by bread alone, but by every word that comes from the mouth of God.'"

Then the devil took Jesus to Jerusalem and placed him at the very top of the temple. He said to Jesus, "If you are the Son of God, throw yourself off this temple. The scriptures say that God will send angels to save you."

Jesus said, "No. The scriptures say, 'Do not put the Lord your God to the test.' I will not throw myself down from the temple."

Finally, the devil took Jesus to the top of a high mountain, where they could look out and see all the nations in the world. The devil said, "If you will fall down and worship me, I will give you all of these kingdoms."

But Jesus said, "No. Go away, Satan! The scriptures say you should only worship God."

Then the devil went away, and angels appeared and cared for Jesus.

Wonder: How do you think Jesus felt when the devil was near him? I wonder if it was hard to say no. I wonder how Jesus felt when the angels came and cared for him.

Explore

The "year of the Lord's favor" when the "oppressed go free" sounds like Jubilee. Read the story on page 58 (Leviticus 25:8–55). Read or listen to the news to spot good news for poor people.

Jesus brings good news

Luke 4:14–30

When Jesus left the wilderness after being tempted by the devil, he returned to Galilee. He began to teach in the synagogues and everyone praised him. People all over the countryside were talking about him.

Then Jesus came to Nazareth, the town where he had grown up. On the Sabbath, he went to the synagogue. He stood up to read the scripture and the scroll of the prophet Isaiah was given to him. Jesus unrolled the scroll and read:

"The Spirit of the Lord is upon me, because he has anointed me to bring good news to the poor. He has sent me to proclaim release to the captives and recovery of sight to the blind, to let the oppressed go free, to proclaim the year of the Lord's favor."

Then Jesus rolled up the scroll, gave it back, and sat down. Everyone was watching him. He began to speak to the people, saying, "Today this scripture has come true in your hearing."

Everyone was amazed at how well he spoke. They asked each other, "Isn't this the son of Joseph and Mary?"

Jesus continued, "I tell you this, no prophet is accepted in the prophet's own hometown.

"There were many widows in Israel during the prophet Elijah's time, yet Elijah was not sent to them. Instead, he was sent to help a widow in Zarephath in Sidon—a woman who wasn't an Israelite.

"And during the time of the prophet Elisha, there were many lepers in Israel. Yet Elisha healed only Naaman, who was from the enemy country of Syria."

As the crowd began to understand that Jesus was criticizing them, they grew angrier and angrier. Finally they drove him out of the synagogue and out of the town. They led him to a hill so they could throw him off a cliff.

But Jesus slipped through the crowd and continued on his way, teaching and healing people.

Wonder: Why were the people so angry with what Jesus said in the synagogue?

Jesus calls disciples

Mark 1:16–45

Connect

Imagine that Jesus healed you. Who would be the first person you would tell?

One day while Jesus was walking along the Sea of Galilee, he saw Simon and Simon's brother Andrew fishing. Jesus said to them, "Follow me, and I will make you fish for people." Right away, Simon and Andrew stopped fishing and followed Jesus.

Farther on, Jesus saw James and his brother John. They were in their boat fixing fishing nets. Jesus called them, and they left their boat and followed him.

Jesus went to the synagogue in Capernaum and taught. People were amazed. They could tell that Jesus spoke with God's love and power. When a man who was ill began to shout at him, Jesus healed the man.

Then Jesus went to Simon's house, where Simon's mother-in-law was very sick. Jesus took her hand and lifted her up, and she was better right away. That evening the whole city crowded around the door. Jesus healed many people that night.

In the morning, while it was still very dark, Jesus got up and went to a deserted place to pray. Simon and the other friends came looking for him. When they found Jesus, they told him, "Everyone is searching for you."

Jesus answered, "Let's go to other towns so that I can share my message there too. This is what I came to do." So Jesus continued to travel with his friends, teaching and healing people.

One man with leprosy came to him and said, "I know that you can heal me if you choose." Jesus stretched out his hand and touched the man, saying, "I do choose. Be healed!" And immediately the leprosy left the man. Then Jesus sent him away, saying, "Say nothing to anyone; just go to the temple and show the priests that you are cured."

But the man was too happy and excited to keep quiet. He told everyone he met about what Jesus had done for him. Soon Jesus couldn't go into towns anymore, because when he did, many people crowded around him. So Jesus stayed out in the country, and people came from all over to hear his teaching and to be healed.

Wonder: I wonder what made those fishermen leave their jobs and follow Jesus.

Explore

It was hard work dragging in fish and repairing nets, but many people didn't think these workers were very special. The Sea of Galilee boat (left), also known as the Jesus boat, is an ancient fishing boat from this time period.

Explore

A steward's job is to oversee a family or a household. In this story the steward made sure the food and drink was good before serving the guests. Try being the steward at your next family meal!

Jars discovered at Kfar Kana, Galilee, the possible location of Cana where the wedding took place

As Jesus was beginning to travel through the countryside, he went to the town of Cana, in Galilee, to attend a wedding. His mother, Mary, and his disciples were also there.

The guests were enjoying the wedding feast when the servants discovered that the wine had run out. Mary said to Jesus, "They have no wine." Jesus answered her in a puzzling way, "That is not our concern. My time has not yet come."

But Mary was sure that Jesus could help. She said to the servants, "Do whatever he tells you."

There were six large stone water jars standing nearby. Each one could hold twenty or thirty gallons! Jesus said to the servants, "Fill those jars with water." The servants filled each jar right up to the very top.

Then Jesus said, "Take some out and give it to the chief steward." So they did, and the steward tasted it. It was not water anymore; it was wine!

The steward didn't know where this wine had come from, but he knew that it was good. He called the bridegroom over to him and said, "Everyone else serves the best wine first and saves the worst wine for later. But you have kept the best wine until now."

Turning the water into wine was a sign of Jesus' glory, a sign that he was God's chosen one. His disciples saw this, and they believed in him.

Wonder: Imagine being a servant looking for wine and being told to fill enormous jars with water.

Explore

Jesus said that God's spirit gives new life. It is like being born all over again! What things do new babies learn? What are some things that we learn from Jesus?

Connect
The Spirit of God blows like a wind through our world. Pay attention each day to see where God's spirit brings goodness and new life. Share what you notice with others.

Nicodemus visits Jesus

John 3:1–21

Nicodemus, a teacher in Israel, visited Jesus one night. Nicodemus said, "Rabbi, we know you have come from God. No one can do the signs you've been doing unless God is with him."

Jesus talked with Nicodemus about finding the kingdom of God. "You must be born into God's kingdom. That's the way to start."

"How can a grownup be born?" Nicodemus wondered. "Can I become a baby all over again?"

"God's spirit gives new life," Jesus answered. "It is like being born—making a fresh start. What is born of human flesh is flesh, and what is born of the Spirit of God is spirit.

"God's spirit is like the wind. It blows where it chooses. You can hear it, but you don't know where it comes from or where it goes. In the same way, you cannot see the Spirit of God, but it is there."

Nicodemus said, "How can this be? I don't understand."

Jesus answered him, "You are a teacher of Israel, and yet you do not understand these things?"

Jesus said, "God loves the world. God sent the Son into the world to save the world. The Son of God has brought light into the world. This light is for everyone."

Nicodemus had come walking in the dark to see Jesus. But Jesus said, "If you do what is good and true, you are walking in God's light."

Wonder: Why did Nicodemus go to visit Jesus at night?

Jesus and the Samaritan woman

John 4:1–42

Connect

Get yourself a glass of water. As you drink the water, imagine sharing water with Jesus at the well.

The well at Sychar, in the land of Samaria, was hundreds of years old. Over the years, many people had come to get water and rest beside the well.

Jesus and his disciples were passing through Samaria, and in the middle of the day they came to the well. Jesus was tired and sat down to rest. The disciples went into the village to buy food.

As Jesus rested, a Samaritan woman came to fill her water jar. Jesus said to her, "Give me a drink." The woman was surprised and said, "You're asking me, a woman of Samaria, for a drink?" She and Jesus both knew that Jews did not share things with Samaritans.

Jesus answered, "Do you know about God's gifts? Do you know who is asking you for water? If you had known, you would have asked me for living water, and I would have given it to you."

"Sir, you have no bucket," the woman said. "Where would you get this living water? Are you greater than our ancestor Jacob who gave us this well?"

"Everyone who drinks from this well will be thirsty again," Jesus told her. "But people who drink the water that I give will never be thirsty. That water will become a spring inside them, gushing up into new life forever."

The woman said, "Sir, give me this water."

Jesus said, "Go, call your husband and come back." The woman answered, "I have no husband."

"You are right," said Jesus. "You have had five husbands, and the man you are with now is not your husband."

The woman was amazed that Jesus knew all about her. She sat by the well with Jesus and they talked about God. The woman said, "I know that the Messiah, our Savior, is coming."

Jesus said, "I am the Messiah."

The woman left her jar by the well and ran back to the city to tell others about Jesus. Everyone she told wanted to meet him too. Jesus stayed in Samaria for two days. During that time, many Samaritans came to believe that Jesus was the Messiah.

Wonder: I wonder how there could be a spring of living water inside me.

GALILEE

Great
Sea

Nazareth

SAMARIA

Sychar

Jerusalem

JUDEA

Explore

Jesus loved and valued all kinds of people including Samaritans and tax collectors. Look online to find out about Friends Without Borders. Read or write letters to make friends in another country.

Explore

Thinking of the friends in the story, make a list of words that describe a good friend. Find ways to show your friends that you care about them this week.

Great Sea

GALILEE

Capernaum

Sea of Galilee

Nazareth

SAMARIA

The man through the roof

Mark 2:1–12

Jesus went from town to town. He taught people about God and healed people who were sick. Crowds followed him wherever he went.

When Jesus returned to his home in Capernaum, the news spread quickly: "Jesus is back!" People ran to see Jesus. So many people crowded into Jesus' house that there was no room for them, not even outside the door.

Four friends came carrying another friend who could not walk. They wanted to bring him to Jesus, but they could not get inside the house. That did not stop them, though. They really wanted their friend to see Jesus.

The friends climbed up onto the roof and dug a hole through it. They took the mat the man was lying on and lowered it through the hole! Now the man was right next to Jesus.

When Jesus saw how the friends believed in him, he said to the man, "You are forgiven."

There were some leaders sitting there and they heard what Jesus said. They wondered, "How can he talk like this? Who does he think he is? Only God can say, 'You are forgiven.'"

Jesus knew what they were thinking and saying. He said to them, "I will show you that I have authority from God." He turned to the man who could not walk and said, "Stand up, take your mat, and go to your home."

Immediately, the man stood up, picked up his mat, and left. The people were amazed. They said, "We have never seen anything like this! Praise God!"

Wonder: Picture the large group of people who wanted to see and hear Jesus.

193

Beatitudes

Matthew 5:1–12

Connect

Jesus tells us how we can be blessed and be a blessing to others. Make a string of beads, one bead for each blessing. Pray through the blessings, asking God to help you with each one.

Jesus moved around the countryside of Galilee telling people about God's love. Great crowds followed him. One day, when Jesus saw the crowd before him, he went up the mountain. When he sat down, the disciples came to him and he taught them. He said:

"Blessed are the poor in spirit, for theirs is the kingdom of heaven. You are blessed when you depend on God.

"Blessed are those who mourn, for they will be comforted. God will comfort you when you are sad.

"Blessed are the meek, for they will inherit the earth. You will be happy when you do not always need to have your own way.

"Blessed are those who hunger and thirst for righteousness, for they will be filled. When you really want to follow God's way, God will be with you.

"Blessed are the merciful, for they will receive mercy. When you are kind to others, you will also feel God's love.

"Blessed are the pure in heart, for they will see God. When you follow God with your whole heart, you will see God at work all around you.

"Blessed are the peacemakers, for they will be called children of God. You are part of God's family when you show love to everyone.

"Blessed are those who are persecuted for righteousness' sake, for theirs is the kingdom of heaven. People may be mean to you or tell lies about you when you do what is right. Know that you belong to God."

Wonder: I wonder why Jesus said that sad people are blessed.

Explore

We are often told that we should try to be number one and get our own way. How do you think our world would be different if we tried to live in the way that Jesus taught us to?

Love your enemies

Matthew 5:38–48

Jesus taught the disciples how to follow God's way. Jesus' ideas were different from other ways people had been taught to act.

Jesus said, "You have heard it said, 'If someone does something bad to you, do the same thing back.' But I say to you, it is better to love your enemy. If anyone hits you on the right cheek, turn the other cheek toward that person. If someone wants to take your coat, give up your cloak also. And if anyone makes you walk a mile, don't stop there: walk on another mile."

Jesus went on, "You have heard it said, 'Love your neighbor and hate your enemy.' But I say to you, love your enemies as well as your neighbors! Pray for the people who treat you badly. This is how you show that you are children of God.

"God makes the sun shine on everything. It shines on things that are bad and it shines on things that are good. God makes the rain fall on everyone. It rains on people who follow God's ways, and it rains on people who don't follow God's ways.

"God wants you to love everyone. If you are only kind to those who are kind to you, what good is that? Anyone can do that! If you talk only to the people in your family and your community, how are you showing God's love? God wants us to be different. We are God's sons and daughters. Let's live like God's children, and love every-one as God loves."

Wonder: What would the world be like if the sun would shine only on people doing something kind?

Connect

Read Proverbs 25:21–22. How does this proverb connect to what Jesus is saying? Jesus' examples seem to say, "Don't hit back but also don't be bullied. We are all created in God's image. Choose love, not hatred." Pray: *God, help me show love today even in tough situations.*

Explore

Fasting doesn't have to be about giving up food. You can also decide to give up something else, like watching TV or playing video games one day a week. The important thing is to find a way to spend more time with God.

Give, pray, fast

Matthew 6:1–18

Connect

Read over the prayer Jesus taught his disciples and make up actions to fit with each part of the prayer. Now you can pray using your entire body! Below are some words in American Sign Language.

Heaven

Holy

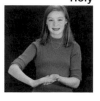

Kingdom

Bread

Forgiven

Jesus was always teaching his disciples about how to follow God. He told them again and again that it is important to speak and act honestly and not do things just to impress other people.

He talked to them about giving to others. He said, "It is good to give offerings and share what you have with others. But be careful not to make a show of your giving. If you make a big deal about what you give, people might praise you rather than God. So do your giving quietly; God will know what you have done."

He talked about how to pray. He said, "When you talk to God, keep it simple. Don't try to impress God or anyone else by praying loudly so everyone can hear you. Find a quiet place where you can just focus on God. God will hear your honest words and thoughts.

"Don't try to use lots of words when you pray. Pray like this:

"Our Father in heaven, hallowed be your name.
Your kingdom come. Your will be done, on earth as it is in heaven.
Give us this day our daily bread.
And forgive us our debts, as we also have forgiven our debtors.
And do not bring us to the time of trial, but rescue us from the evil one.

"When you forgive others, God will forgive you."

He talked about fasting, or giving up something like food, in order to spend time with God.

"If you fast, don't look gloomy and go around with your face all twisted up so everyone notices. Just wash your face and comb your hair as usual. Your fasting should be a private thing. God will know what you have done."

Wonder: I wonder what the disciples prayed about. Do you think some of their prayers might be the same as yours?

Explore

When we share with each other it is more likely that everyone will have the food and clothing they need. How have others helped you? How can you help others know that God cares for them?

Connect

Are there times when you worry? When you are worried or afraid, use your imagination and invite God to sit with you and hear your worries. How does God respond?

Don't worry

Matthew 6:25–34

Jesus said to his followers:

Do you worry about yourself: what you will eat and what you will wear? Isn't life more than food and clothing?

Look at the birds of the air. Do the birds worry about growing grain to eat? They do not—but God still cares for their needs.

Think about the lilies of the field. They grow and bloom without trying. Yet even King Solomon in all his glory was not clothed as beautifully as these flowers.

God cares for the birds. God clothes the flowers and grasses of the field, which are alive today and gone tomorrow. How much more will God care for you!

Don't worry about what you will eat or drink or say, "What will I wear?" God knows that you need all these things.

Do your best for God's kingdom. Make following God the most important thing. The rest will fall into place. Do not worry about what might happen tomorrow. Today's troubles are enough for today. Trust in God's care. God knows what you need.

Wonder: How do birds search for their food? Think about plants. How do they get what they need to grow?

Explore

During the day, go outside and take a look at the foundation of your house or apartment. What does the foundation do for your home?

Connect

Find a small rock that fits nicely in your palm. Write one important word from Jesus on the rock with a marker. Keep the rock by your bed as a reminder of a strong foundation.

Jesus said:

Everyone who hears me and follows my teachings is like a wise builder who built a house on a foundation of rock.

The rain fell.

The floods came.

The winds began to blow against the house.

The house did not fall because it had been built on a foundation of solid rock.

But everyone who hears me and does not follow my words is like a foolish builder who built a house on sand.

The rain fell.

The floods came.

The winds began to blow against the house.

And it fell—and great was its fall!

Wonder: What are some of the teachings that Jesus wants us to hear and follow?

The sower and the seed

Mark 4:1–20

Connect

Pray: *God, you are the good farmer. Help me to grow strong and healthy in your field, producing lots of fruit.*

A crowd gathered around Jesus as he stood by the sea. There were so many people that Jesus got into a boat and sat there, while everyone crowded around on the shore. Jesus began to tell a story.

"Listen!" he said. "A farmer went out to sow some seeds. As the farmer sowed, some seeds fell on the path, and birds came and ate them up.

"Other seeds fell on rocky ground where there was not much soil. Since the soil was shallow and warm, the seeds sprouted quickly, but they couldn't put down roots. When the sun rose, the sprouts were scorched. Without roots, the plants withered away and died.

"Other seeds fell among thorns. The thorns grew up all around the seedlings, and choked them out.

"Other seeds fell onto good soil. Those seeds grew and grew until the farmer could harvest the grain. One seed produced a hundred times its weight!

"Listen!" Jesus said. "If you have ears to hear, listen!"

After Jesus finished teaching by the seashore, the disciples asked him about the story. They weren't sure what he meant. Jesus told them, "The seeds are like God's message. Sometimes people don't hear or act on these words. That is like seed that falls on the path or on rocky ground or among thorns. Not much ever comes of this.

"But those who hear God's word and follow God's ways are like the plants in good soil. They grow and produce fruit—a great harvest of goodness and love."

"Listen! If you have ears to hear, listen!"

Wonder: Imagine being the farmer, sowing your seeds in different kinds of soil. Picture yourself kneeling down in the different kinds of soil and looking closely at how the plants grow.

Explore

Jesus often told parables about growing food and caring for animals—things from people's everyday lives. What is a part of your daily life that Jesus might tell a parable about today?

Explore

Page through the Gospel of Matthew and notice that it often says "kingdom of heaven." The Jewish people thought God's name was too holy to repeat, so Matthew said "kingdom of heaven" instead of "kingdom of God."

Hidden treasure

Matthew 13:44–50

Jesus told stories to show what God's kingdom is like:
The kingdom of heaven is like a treasure hidden in a field. A worker who finds the treasure will hide it away again. Then the worker will sell everything to get enough money to buy the field where the treasure is hidden.

Jesus told another story:
The kingdom of heaven is like a merchant who travels around looking for wonderful pearls to buy. When the merchant finds one very valuable pearl, the merchant will sell everything to buy that one precious pearl.

And Jesus said:
The kingdom of heaven is also like a big fishing net that was thrown into the sea and caught all kinds of fish. When the net was full, those who were fishing pulled it onto land, sat down, and divided out the good and bad fish. They put the good fish into baskets and threw out the bad fish. This is what it will be like at the end of the age.

Wonder: How is God's kingdom like a treasure? How is it like a fishing net full of fish?

Jesus heals two daughters

Mark 5:21–43

Connect

Jesus cared for people who needed healing. Think of someone you know who is sick. How might you help them to feel better?

Jesus took a boat and crossed the sea, and a huge crowd gathered around him on the shore. Jairus, a leader of the local synagogue, knelt down at Jesus' feet. "My daughter is dying," said Jairus. He begged Jesus, "Please come and lay your hands on her so that she will get well." So Jesus went with Jairus.

The crowd surrounded Jesus and followed along. In the crowd there was a woman who had been sick for twelve years. She had gone to many doctors, but instead of getting better, she had gotten worse. She had heard about Jesus and she said to herself, "If I can just touch his clothes, I will be made well." So she came up behind Jesus and touched his cloak. Immediately she felt in her body that she was healed.

Jesus knew that power had gone out from him. He looked around the crowd and asked, "Who touched my clothes?" Jesus' disciples said, "How can you ask that? Look at this huge crowd. Lots of people are touching you."

But the woman came forward, even though she was very frightened. She knelt down at Jesus' feet and told him her story. Jesus said, "Daughter, your faith has made you well. Go in peace, and be healed."

While Jesus was speaking with the women, some people came from Jairus's house. They said, "Your daughter has died. Don't bother the teacher anymore." But Jesus heard what they said, and told Jairus, "Do not fear, only believe."

Jesus and some of the disciples continued on to the house of Jairus. Jesus went in, took the child by the hand, and said, "*Talitha cum*," which means, "Little girl, get up!" Immediately the girl got up and began to walk around.

All the people there were amazed. Jesus ordered them not to tell anyone what he had done. Then he asked them to give the girl something to eat.

Wonder: I wonder why the woman believed that touching Jesus' clothes would heal her.

Explore

At times, people who were sick were separated from their communities and no one would touch them. Jesus often surprised the crowds by touching people who were sick, showing God's love. Do we have "untouchable" people?

Enough food by the sea

Mark 6:30–44

Connect

When we share, wonderful things happen. Have you been a part of a fundraiser to end hunger? Pray: *God, help us to care about others so that there can be enough for all.*

The disciples of Jesus went out traveling and teaching. Then they came back together again to tell Jesus what they had been doing. They were so busy, with many people coming and going, that they did not even have time to eat. Jesus said to them, "Come away with me to a deserted place where you can rest for a while." So they went away by boat to a place where they could be by themselves.

But many people recognized them and saw where they were headed. They hurried to that place on foot while Jesus and the disciples went by boat. When Jesus and the disciples got to the other shore, a crowd of people had already arrived.

Jesus felt pity in his heart for all these people, for he saw that they were like sheep without a shepherd. Instead of sending them away, he began to teach them.

Then it grew late, and the disciples came to Jesus. "Send the people away to the nearby towns," they said. "Then they will be able to buy themselves food to eat."

Jesus answered, "You give them something to eat."

The disciples were shocked. "How can we buy food for all these people?" they asked.

Jesus said, "Go and see how much bread you have." The disciples found five loaves of bread and two fish.

Then Jesus told the disciples to have the people sit down in groups on the green grass. The people, five thousand of them in all, sat down in groups of hundreds and fifties.

Jesus took the fish and the loaves of bread, looked up to heaven, and blessed the food. He broke the loaves into pieces and gave those to the disciples. He divided the fish among them as well.

The disciples passed out the food to all the groups of people. Everyone ate until they were full. Then the disciples collected what was left—and amazingly, there were twelve baskets full of bread and fish.

Wonder: I wonder why the people were so determined to be with Jesus.

Explore

This story is also told in Matthew 14:13-21; Luke 9:12-17; and John 6:4-13, but they're not all the same. Find the version where a young boy shares his food with the crowd.

Loaves and Fishes mosaic from Tabgah, Israel

Jesus walks on water

Mark 6:45–52

Connect

How do you feel when you're afraid? Sometimes it can feel like there is a storm inside of us. The next time you're afraid, breathe slowly and invite Jesus to calm your heart.

After Jesus fed the huge crowd of people, he sent his disciples in the boat to go across to Bethsaida. Jesus said farewell to the crowd and then went up on a mountain to pray.

When evening came, the boat was out on the sea, and Jesus was alone on the land. He saw that a wind had come up and the disciples were straining at the oars, trying to keep the boat on course.

Jesus came towards the boat, walking on the sea. When the disciples saw him, they cried out in fear; they thought they were seeing a ghost.

But immediately Jesus spoke to them and said, "Take heart, it is I; do not be afraid." Then Jesus got into the boat with the disciples and the wind stopped.

The disciples were completely amazed. Even with all they had seen, they did not understand about Jesus and his power.

Wonder: I wonder why Jesus stayed behind to pray.

Explore

Many stories and psalms in the Bible show God's power over creation. Read Psalm 33:6–9.

Explore

Almost all the other stories of Jesus take place in Galilee, Samaria, or Judea. Tyre was a powerful port city. The Roman ruins shown in this picture can help us imagine Jesus in this unusual setting.

Connect

The woman reminded Jesus that God's love is for everyone. How can you show this in your life?

Jesus heals a little girl

Mark 7:24–30

Crowds gathered wherever Jesus went. So Jesus traveled outside Jewish territory to the region of Tyre. He stayed in a house and hoped that no one would know he was there. But he could not escape attention for long.

Soon a woman whose daughter was sick came to Jesus. She was Syrophoenician—a Gentile, not a Jew. She knelt down at Jesus' feet and begged him to heal her little girl.

At first Jesus did not say yes. Instead he said to the woman, "The children should be fed first. It isn't fair to take their food and throw it to the dogs."

The woman understood what that meant. Jesus was saying that his job was to heal his own kind of people, the Jews.

But the woman did not give up. She said, "Sir, even dogs under the table eat the children's crumbs."

Jesus told the woman, "Because you have said this, you may go. Your daughter has been healed."

When the woman got home, she found her daughter resting on her bed. She was well again!

Wonder: I wonder why Jesus changed his mind.

Explore

Among other ancient peoples, only the wealthy had days of rest. But Jewish Sabbath rules said that ordinary people, servants, and even donkeys should rest one day of every week (Deuteronomy 5:14).

Connect

What do you do differently on Saturday or Sunday than on other days of the week? What can you do to help others on those days?

Healing on the Sabbath

Luke 6:1–11

One Sabbath, Jesus' disciples plucked some heads of grain, rubbed them in their hands, and ate them. Some of the Pharisees asked Jesus, "Why are you breaking Sabbath rules?"

Jesus said, "Do you remember the story about what David and his friends did when they were very hungry? David entered the house of God and took bread that only priests are supposed to eat. Are rules more important than people? What would King David think?"

On another Sabbath, Jesus was teaching in the synagogue. There was a man in the congregation with a withered hand. The religious leaders watched Jesus closely to see if he would heal on the Sabbath.

Jesus told the man to stand up. Jesus looked around and asked, "Is it lawful to do good on the Sabbath? Should we save life or destroy it?"

No one answered. So Jesus told the man to stretch out his hand. The man's hand was restored!

The Pharisees were furious that Jesus had healed someone on the Sabbath.

Wonder: Why were there rules about what you could and could not do on the Sabbath? Why did breaking the rules upset the Pharisees?

Explore

Take a look at the story of Jesus' baptism on page 1/8.
How is that story similar to this one?

218

Transfiguration

Matthew 17:1–9; Mark 9:2–9; Luke 9:28–36

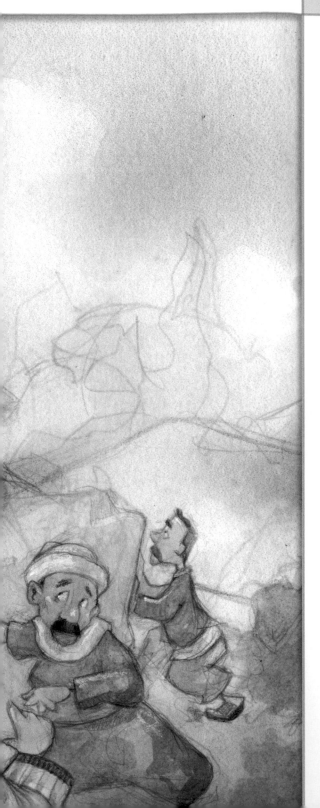

Jesus took his disciples Peter, James, and John up to a high mountain to pray. There, in the quiet, something amazing happened. Right before the disciples' eyes, Jesus changed. His face shone like the sun, and his clothes became dazzling white.

Suddenly two other people appeared and started talking with Jesus. They were Moses, the great leader who had helped bring the Israelites out of slavery in Egypt, and Elijah, one of God's prophets from long ago.

Peter said to Jesus, "Teacher, it is good for us to be here. If you want me to, I will build three houses here, one for you, one for Moses, and one for Elijah."

While Peter was talking, a bright cloud passed over them and they heard a voice saying, "This is my Son, the Beloved. I am very pleased with him. Listen to him!"

When the disciples heard the voice, they were very frightened and they fell down on the ground.

But Jesus came and gently touched them, saying, "Get up. Do not be afraid." When the disciples looked up, only Jesus was there with them.

As they came down the mountain, Jesus told his companions, "Do not tell anyone about this vision until after my resurrection." And Peter, James, and John kept silent, as Jesus had asked, until later.

Wonder: I wonder why Moses and Elijah appeared on the mountain.

Explore

Draw a simple map showing places in your world (home, school, church, parks). Put red dots at the places where you feel loved without needing to be "the best" or "the most important."

220

Remember a time when you wished that you were the best or the most important. Know that you are important and loved by Jesus just because you're you.

True greatness

Mark 9:33–37

Jesus and his disciples walked to Capernaum. When they got there, Jesus asked, "What were you arguing about on the way?"

The disciples got very quiet. They had been arguing about which of them was the most important.

Jesus sat down and said, "Whoever wants to be first must be the last of all and the servant of everyone."

Then Jesus picked up a little child. Holding the child in his arms, he told the disciples, "Whoever welcomes a child welcomes me. And whoever welcomes me welcomes God, who sent me."

Wonder: Imagine the disciples, arguing about who was the most important. What might they have said to each other?

Explore

In Jesus' time people looked down on Samaritans. *Samaritan* and *good* were not words that people said together. Today, Jesus might tell the story of the good _____. (*Fill in the blank*.)

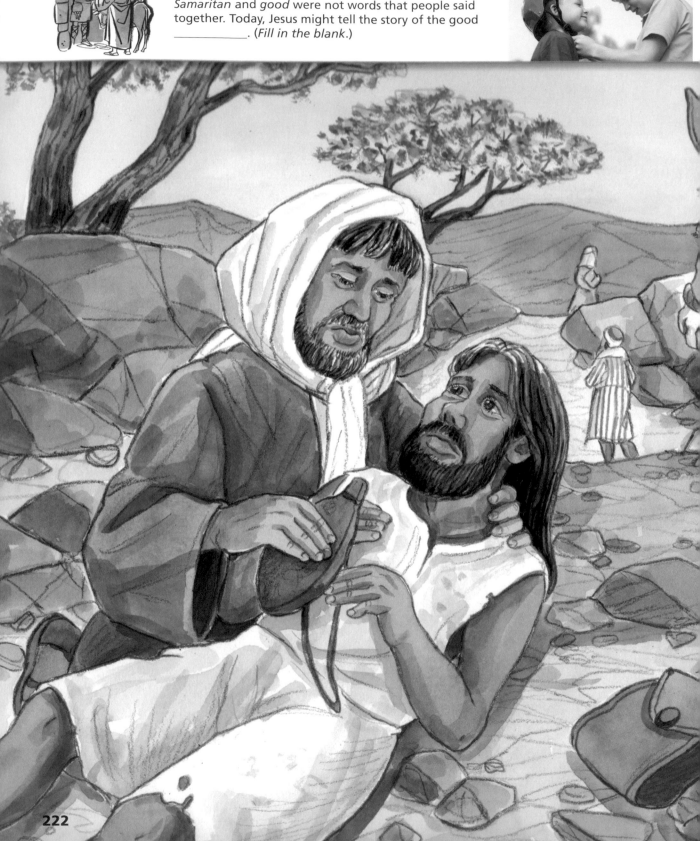

222

The good Samaritan

Luke 10:25–37

A lawyer wanted to test Jesus, so he asked, "What do I need to do to receive life with God?" Jesus asked, "What does the law say?"

"You shall love the Lord your God with all your heart, and with all your soul, and with all your strength, and with all your mind; and your neighbor as yourself."

Jesus said, "You gave the right answer. This is exactly what you should do."

Then the lawyer asked, "But who is my neighbor?" This time, Jesus answered with a story.

"On the steep and lonely road from Jerusalem to Jericho, a traveler lay beside the road. He needed help. Robbers had beaten him. They had taken his money and clothes.

"A priest came walking down the road. He looked at the hurt man—and quickly walked by on the other side of the road.

"A Levite, an assistant to the priests, came walking down the road and saw the man. He also quickly walked by on the other side.

"A Samaritan passing by also saw the man lying by the road. He stopped, came over, and bent down to help the man. He put oil on the man's cuts and bandaged up his wounds. Then the Samaritan put the hurt man on his animal and took him to an inn that was nearby. The man needed good food and rest to get better.

"The next day the Samaritan traveler gave money to the innkeeper and said, 'Please take good care of this man. If you spend more than this, I will pay you back the next time I am here.'"

After telling this story, Jesus asked, "Which of the people was a good neighbor?"

The lawyer answered, "The one who showed kindness."

Jesus said, "Go and do the same."

Wonder: I wonder why the priest and Levite just walked past the injured man. I wonder why the Samaritan decided to stop.

223

Mary and Martha

Luke 10:38–42

Connect
Following Jesus means both doing things to help others, and sitting and listening. What kinds of work do we do to help others? How can we quietly listen to God?

Martha and her sister Mary invited Jesus to their home. Mary sat at Jesus' feet and listened to him talk. But Martha was busy making the food, setting the table, and serving people. Martha worried about all that had to be done for their guests.

Martha said, "Jesus, don't you care that my sister has left me to do all the work by myself? Tell her then to help me!"

"Martha, Martha," Jesus answered, "You are worried and upset about many things, but one thing is most important. Mary has chosen what is better and I will not take it away from her."

Wonder: Imagine being Martha, trying to do all the work for your guests.

Explore

In the ancient world, women were expected to serve others. They were rarely allowed to sit and learn from teachers. But Jesus welcomed women as learners, teachers, and leaders.

Mustard seed and yeast

Luke 13:18–21

Connect

Jesus told lots of stories describing God's kingdom. What do you think the kingdom of God is like? Create your own short parable.

One Sabbath day, Jesus was teaching in a synagogue. He asked, "What is God's kingdom like?"

Jesus answered his own question with two stories, or parables:

"The kingdom of God is like a mustard seed. Someone took this tiny seed and planted it in a garden. The seed sprouted and grew until it became a tree. This tree was so big that birds could make nests in its branches.

"The kingdom of God is like yeast that a woman added to flour. She mixed and mixed until the yeast and the flour were completely blended together. Then, the flour was leavened, ready to be turned into dough and made into delicious and nourishing bread."

Wonder: Imagine that you are a mustard seed. Curl up your body like a tiny seed. Then try moving around in different ways to become a tree.

Explore

Most bread (and pizza dough!) is made with yeast. Find an adult who bakes bread and ask that person to show you how yeast works.

227

Explore

Jesus says that a good host doesn't just invite family and close friends to the party. Can you think of people you don't know very well that you could invite to your home?

Connect

Think of a time when you were invited to a party. Think of a time when you were left out. Pray: *God, thank you that all people are invited to be a part of your kingdom.*

Come to the banquet

Luke 14:1–24

Jesus and many others were invited to the home of an important Pharisee. Jesus noticed how all the guests wanted to sit in the places of honor. He said:

"When you're invited to a wedding banquet, don't sit in the places reserved for honored guests. You don't know—the host might come and ask you to move to the lowest place to make room for a more important person. Instead, when you are invited to a banquet, take a seat at the lowest place. Then, it could be that your host will come to you and say, 'Friend, move up higher.'"

Jesus also had some words for the Pharisee who had invited him to this dinner:

"When you give a dinner, don't invite only your good friends, relatives, or rich neighbors. These people easily pay you back by inviting you to another dinner. Instead, when you give a banquet, invite people who are poor, disabled, and blind. You will be blessed for inviting people who cannot pay you back."

Then Jesus told a story:

A man planned a splendid dinner and invited many neighbors and friends. When the dinner was ready, he sent someone to say, "Come; everything is ready now."

But instead of coming, the people all sent excuses.

"Sorry, I can't come. I bought some land and I have to go see it."

"I bought five pairs of oxen. I'll have to go try them. Sorry, I won't be able to come."

"Sorry, I've just gotten married. I can't come."

The host was angry at hearing all these poor excuses. He told the servant, "Go out at once to the streets and lanes of the town. Bring in people who are poor, disabled, blind, and lame."

The servant did what the host ordered, and brought many people in for the dinner. After all these people were seated there was still room for more. "Go out and find more strangers and bring them to the table, too," said the host. "Fill the house. Everyone is welcome at my banquet."

Wonder: Imagine a banquet with Jesus. Draw a picture of the party.

Explore

Sometimes it's hard to know what is right and wrong—especially when something is right to do in one place but wrong in another! God gives us families, friends, and teachers who can help us make good decisions.

Searching for the lost

Luke 15:1–10

All kinds of people came to listen to Jesus. Some were people who were not following the laws of Moses or were causing harm to other people. Some religious leaders did not like this. They grumbled and said, "This man Jesus welcomes sinners and eats with them."

Jesus answered the leaders with two stories:

"Imagine a shepherd who has one hundred sheep. What if one of them gets lost? The shepherd will leave the other sheep and hunt until the lost sheep is found. When the shepherd finds the sheep, he will carry it home, rejoicing. When he gets home, he will call out to friends and neighbors saying, 'Rejoice with me, for I have found my sheep that was lost.'

"It's like that when someone turns from wrong. There is more joy in heaven because of one person who is sorry for the mistakes he or she has done, than over ninety-nine people who are sure they haven't done anything wrong.

"Or, think about a woman who has ten precious coins. If she loses one of them, she will light her lamp and sweep the whole house. She will search carefully in every corner until she finds the coin. Then she will call to her friends and neighbors, 'Celebrate with me, for I have found the coin that I lost.'

"This is the way God's angels celebrate when someone turns from doing wrong to following God's ways."

Wonder: Picture the lost sheep being found. I wonder if the sheep has a name. I wonder if you have ever felt like that sheep.

Explore

Feasts were important ways for people to celebrate and give thanks to God. Plan a special feast with your family to celebrate God's goodness and love.

The loving father

Luke 15:11–32

Jesus told this parable:

Once there was a man who had two sons. The sons knew that when their father died, they would inherit his property.

The older son was a hard worker on his father's farm. The younger son did not want to stay on the farm and work. He said to his father, "Give me my share of your property now."

The father divided his property and gave the younger son his share. A few days later the younger son gathered all he had and traveled to a faraway country. There, he spent all his money. He had to take a job with a farmer, who sent him out to the fields to feed pigs. He was so hungry that he would gladly have eaten the pigs' food.

The son said to himself, "My father's workers have more bread than they can eat, and here I am, dying of hunger. I will go to my father and tell him I'm sorry. I'll ask him to hire me as one of his workers."

So the son set off for home. While he was still far off down the road, the father saw him. He ran to his son, hugged him, and kissed him. The son said, "Father, I have done so many bad things. I am not good enough to be called your son anymore."

But the father called out, "Bring out a robe for my son. Bring sandals for his feet, and a ring for his finger. We're going to have a feast!" And everyone began to celebrate.

The older son came in from the fields and heard the noise from the party. When he found out what was going on, he was very angry. He said to his father, "This is not fair. I've worked hard and you've never given me a party. My brother spent all his money and you're giving a feast for him!"

The father replied, "Son, you are always with me, and all that I have is yours. But now we must celebrate. Your brother was lost to us, and now he has been found."

Wonder: How do you feel about what the father did?

233

Jesus heals blindness

John 9:1–41

Connect

Jesus used spit and mud to heal the man's eyes. What do doctors or healers use to help you when you are sick?

There was a man who had been born blind. One day, as Jesus and his disciples were walking along, they saw this man. "Teacher," the disciples asked, "why is this man blind? Did he sin or did his parents sin?" Jesus answered, "No one sinned. This man was born blind and now people will see how great God is."

Then Jesus bent down and spat on the ground to make some mud. He spread the mud on the man's eyes. "Go wash in the pool of Siloam," he said. The man went away to do as Jesus said and soon came running back. He could see!

People were surprised when they saw him. "Isn't this the man who used to sit and beg?" they asked each other. "Yes, it is that man!" said one. "No," said another, "it's just someone who looks like him."

The man kept saying, "I am the man!" He told the people about Jesus, the mud, and washing in the pool.

Some religious leaders said, "This healer cannot be from God because he doesn't obey the Sabbath laws." Other leaders disagreed. "He must be from God because he healed this man."

The leaders sent for the man's parents. "Is this your son?" they asked. "Yes," said the parents, "and he was born blind. We don't know how it is that he can see now. You had better ask him."

So the leaders turned again to the man. "Tell the truth! Who is this Jesus?"

"All I know," answered the man, "is that I was blind, but now I can see."

The leaders asked again how he had been healed. He answered, "I told you before and you didn't believe me. That man named Jesus did an amazing thing—something that has never been done since the world began. This could not have happened without God's power."

The leaders were angry at this answer and they made the man leave the temple. Later Jesus found the man and asked, "Do you believe in the Son of man?" The man worshiped Jesus and said, "Lord, I believe."

Wonder: I wonder why the leaders refused to believe that Jesus could heal the man.

Explore

The leaders didn't believe the man's story of healing and so they treated him badly. How can we love people when we don't agree?

235

Jesus the Good Shepherd

John 10:1–18

Jesus told a story to help people understand him:

"The shepherd comes to the gate of the sheepfold and calls the sheep. The sheep hear the voice calling them, and they are not afraid because they know their own shepherd's voice. Anyone who enters the sheepfold in a different way is a thief, not the shepherd.

"The shepherd calls each sheep by name, and one by one they follow the shepherd out of the sheepfold. When all the sheep have come out, the shepherd goes ahead of them. The sheep follow because they know the shepherd's voice. They would not follow a stranger because they do not know the stranger's voice. But they will follow the shepherd."

Jesus continued, "I am the Good Shepherd. The good shepherd will even die to protect the sheep.

"If someone is paid to take care of the sheep, that worker is not the shepherd. If the worker is in charge of the sheep, and a wolf comes, that person will run away.

"The good shepherd does not run away. The shepherd stays to protect the sheep no matter what the danger is.

"I am the Good Shepherd. I know my own and my own know me.

"I have other sheep, too, who do not belong to this sheepfold. I must call them also, so there will be one flock and one shepherd. This is why God loves me, because I am willing to give up my life for my sheep."

Wonder: How is Jesus like a good shepherd?

236

Explore

Sheep herding isn't a very common job anymore. Find a book or do some Internet research to learn more about what it was like to be a shepherd in Bible times and what it is like today.

Connect

How have you felt pushed aside? How have you felt welcomed and loved by others? Know that Jesus always loves you.

Explore

Jesus turned things upside down by caring for children, women, the poor, and the sick, even when many people did not. Draw or list ten children you know. How can you bless them?

Jesus blesses the children

Mark 10:13–16

Jesus traveled into Judea, and crowds gathered around him. As Jesus was teaching them, some Pharisees came. They asked him some difficult questions to test him.

As Jesus was speaking, people began to bring little children to him for his blessing. The disciples spoke sternly to the parents and said, "Take these children away from here."

When Jesus saw this, he was angry with the disciples. "Let the little children come to me, and do not stop them. The kingdom of God belongs to little ones such as these.

"Children can show us the way. Receive God's kingdom the way a child does or you will never enter it."

Then Jesus took the children in his arms and blessed them.

Wonder: Look back over this story. What feelings do you imagine the various characters experienced: Jesus, Pharisees, disciples, parents, children?

The rich man

Mark 10:17–31

Connect

Sometimes getting new toys makes us want even more toys. How might having too many things get in the way of following Jesus?

As Jesus was about to leave on a journey, a man ran up to him.

Kneeling down before Jesus, the man asked, "Good teacher, what must I do to enter the kingdom of God?"

Jesus replied, "Why do you call me good? No one is good but God.

"You know the commandments:

You shall not murder.

Be faithful to your husband or wife.

You shall not steal.

You shall not tell lies about your neighbor.

You shall not cheat.

Honor your father and your mother."

The man said, "Teacher, I have kept all of these rules since I was a child."

Jesus looked at the man and loved him. He said, "Do one more thing. Go, sell what you own, and give the money to help people who are poor. That will bring you treasure in heaven. Then come and follow me."

The man was shocked. He hung his head and went away sadly, for he owned many things.

Then Jesus said to his followers, "It will be hard for people who own many things to enter God's kingdom." He went on, "It would be easier for a camel to go through the eye of a needle than for a rich person to enter God's kingdom."

The disciples were astounded. "Then who can enter God's kingdom?"

Jesus looked at them and said, "For human beings alone, it is impossible. But with God, all things are possible."

Peter spoke up. "Look, we have left everything and followed you."

Jesus replied, "Anyone who leaves home or family or land to follow me will get back even more, even though there will be hard times as well. But many who are first will be last, and the last will be first."

Wonder: Why might it have been hard for someone who owned many things to go and sell them?

Explore

Jesus asked the man to give away his possessions to help people who are poor. What might you be able to give away to help someone else? How does it feel to give things away?

Jesus raises Lazarus

John 11:1–44

Connect
Jesus cried with Mary and Martha. Sometimes very sad things happen in our lives too. Pray: *Jesus, help me to know that you cry with me when I am sad. I am never alone.*

Mary and Martha's brother, Lazarus, was very sick. The sisters sent a message to their friend, Jesus. They were sure he would come and make Lazarus well again.

But when Jesus heard the news he did not leave right away. Instead he said, "This illness will show God's glory."

Two days later, he said, "Let's go to Judea again. Our friend Lazarus has fallen asleep, and I am going to wake him up."

"But Lord," they said, "if Lazarus is sleeping, he will wake up and be all right."

Jesus knew that they did not understand. "Lazarus is dead," he told them. "Let's go to him."

When Jesus finally arrived, Lazarus had been in his tomb for four days. Martha heard that Jesus was coming and ran to meet him on the road. "If you had been here, my brother would not have died. But even now I know God will give you whatever you ask."

Jesus said, "Your brother will rise again. I am the resurrection and the life. Those who believe in me will live, even if they die. Everyone who lives and believes in me will never die. Do you believe this?"

Martha said, "Yes, Lord, I believe."

Then Mary came to Jesus, She knelt at his feet and said, "Lord, if you had been here, my brother would not have died."

Jesus saw her weeping, and he was sad, too. "Where have you laid him?" he asked. They said, "Come and see." Along with Mary and the others, Jesus began to weep.

Jesus arrived at the burial cave, and a stone was lying against it. Jesus said, "Take away the stone."

Martha said, "But, Lord, there will be a bad smell! Lazarus has been dead for four days." Jesus said, "If you believe, you will see the glory of God." So they rolled away the stone.

Jesus looked up and prayed to God. Then he called out loudly, "Lazarus, come out!" Lazarus, who had been dead, walked out of the tomb. Jesus said, "Take the cloth wrappings off him and let him go." Lazarus was alive!

Wonder: I wonder what it means that Jesus is the "resurrection and the life."

GALILEE

Great Sea

Nazareth
SAMARIA

Jerusalem • • Bethany
JUDEA

Explore

In this story God answered Jesus' prayer and Lazarus came from death to life. How do Jesus' teachings lead all of us to better lives together?

Zaccheus responds

Luke 19:1–10

Connect

Zacchaeus made things right, paying back the people that he cheated and giving to the poor. How can you make things right when you do something wrong?

Every day Zacchaeus sat down at his tax booth and collected as much money as he could. It was his work. Every day people frowned at Zacchaeus as he collected money. Every day they looked the other way when they saw him on the street. But every day he also had a little more money: money for a beautiful home and fine food, money for all the things he wanted to own.

Then one day everyone was talking about the news: Jesus was coming to Jericho.

Zacchaeus joined the crowd that was lining the road to see Jesus.

But Zacchaeus was not able to see. So Zacchaeus ran ahead and climbed up into a sycamore fig tree. He knew he would get a good view of Jesus from there.

Finally, Jesus came down the road. As he reached the place where Zacchaeus was, he looked up into the tree and said, "Zacchaeus, hurry and come down. Today I must stay at your house."

Zacchaeus hurried down, delighted to welcome Jesus to his home.

People who had heard what Jesus said began to grumble. Why was Jesus eating with a tax collector like Zacchaeus? Why would Jesus want to be the guest of someone who was a sinner?

"Zacchaeus collects taxes for the Roman government," said someone.

"He got rich from cheating people like me," said another.

While the grumbling was going on outside, Jesus ate with Zacchaeus and talked with him as a friend. Zacchaeus told him, "Look, I will give half of my possessions to the poor. If I have cheated anyone, I will give them four times what I took from them."

Jesus said, "Today salvation has come to this house."

Wonder: I wonder why, out of all the people in Jericho, Jesus chose to eat with Zacchaeus the tax collector.

Explore

Zacchaeus moved from grabbing to sharing, from selfishness to friendship. Read *Four Feet, Two Sandals* by Karen Lynn Williams & Khadra Mohammed or *A Birthday for Frances* by Lillian Hoban.

Left: A very old sycamore tree

Explore

Read Deuteronomy 15:11, a law that Jesus knew well. We still have poor people, as Jesus said. How might we show Jesus our love by how we treat people in need? By our songs and our worship?

Connect

Mary gave a precious gift to Jesus. What are some precious gifts that you have given to others? What precious gifts of love have you received?

Mary anoints Jesus

John 12:1–19

Six days before the Passover, Jesus was invited to have dinner in Bethany at the home of his friends Mary, Martha, and Lazarus. The disciples were there too.

Martha served the meal and Lazarus ate at the table with Jesus. Mary took a pound of expensive perfume made of nard. She came to where Jesus was seated and poured the perfume over Jesus' feet. Then she wiped his feet with her hair. The house was filled with the sweet smell of the perfume.

One of the disciples, Judas Iscariot, wasn't happy about this. He said, "Why didn't you sell this perfume? We could have gotten a lot of money for it. Then we could have used that money to help poor people."

Jesus said to Judas, "Leave Mary alone. She bought the perfume for the day of my burial. You will always have the poor with you, but you won't always have me."

The next day, the great Passover crowd heard that Jesus was coming to Jerusalem. They wanted to see Jesus and they also wanted to see Lazarus, whom Jesus had raised from the dead. They took palm branches and went out to meet him, waving their branches and shouting, "Hosanna! Blessed is the one who comes in the name of the Lord: the King of Israel!" Jesus rode a young donkey, just as the Hebrew scripture said: "Look, your king is coming, sitting on a donkey's colt!"

Jesus' disciples didn't understand. But, seeing the huge crowd, the religious leaders grumbled to one another, "You see? We can't do anything to stop him. Look, the whole world is following him!"

Wonder: I wonder how it feels when our hearts are filled with love. I wonder if Mary just had to do something to show her love.

Explore

Hosanna means "save us, we pray." The Jewish people lived under the rule of the Roman government. They had many hopes that a savior would come like a mighty general and fight for their freedom.

Jesus rides into Jerusalem

Matthew 21:1–11; Mark 11:1–11; Luke 19:28–40

This story is similar to the ending of the previous story. The same story is told a bit differently in each Gospel.

Jesus and his disciples were heading toward Jerusalem.

Near the city Jesus told two of his disciples, "Go into the village ahead of us and you will see a donkey colt tied up. Untie it and bring it back with you. If anyone asks what you are doing, say to them, 'The Lord needs it and will send it right back.'"

The disciples found the colt just as Jesus had said, and brought it back to Jesus. They spread their cloaks on the colt and Jesus sat on it.

So Jesus entered Jerusalem riding on the colt. Some people were so happy and excited about his coming that they spread their cloaks on the road before him. Others cut branches from trees and spread them on the road. Everyone shouted,

"Hosanna to the son of David! Blessed is the king who comes in the name of the Lord! Peace in heaven and glory in the highest heaven!"

Some of the Pharisees in the crowd said, "Teacher, order these people to be quiet."

Jesus answered, "If I silenced these people, the stones themselves would shout out."

Wonder: I wonder what stones would say if they could talk.

Jesus in the temple

**Matthew 21:12–13; Mark 11:15–18;
Luke 19:45–48**

Connect

Many people were selling animals and exchanging money at the temple. What kinds of things happen in your church building when people come to worship?

Jesus went into the temple in Jerusalem. Instead of looking like a house of worship, it looked like a busy marketplace. The courtyard was filled with people buying and selling things. There were people selling doves to present as an offering. There were people exchanging Roman coins for Jewish coins that could be used in the temple.

This made Jesus angry. He walked to where the moneychangers were working, and he threw their tables onto the ground. He did the same thing with the seats of the people who were selling doves. Then he told all the merchants to leave—and to stop carrying their things through the temple.

Jesus said, "Do you remember what the prophets have said?: 'My house is a house of prayer for everyone. But you have made it a den of robbers.'"

Every day after that, Jesus came to the temple and taught. Many people came to hear him and listened carefully to every word he said.

The temple leaders were very unhappy about this. They did not like what Jesus was teaching, and they were afraid of how popular he was with the crowds. They were so angry and afraid that they wished Jesus was dead.

Wonder: Imagine the sounds inside the temple.

Explore

Some people believe that the reason Jesus became upset was because temple merchants were cheating people who had traveled a long distance. Look up "temple tax coins" to learn more.

Jesus refuses to cast stones

John 7:53–8:11

Connect

Instead of rushing to "tell on" someone, we can ask how might this look different if I knew the whole story? Have I ever done wrong? Pray: *Help me to be slow to judge, O God.*

Crowds had been listening to Jesus. At night they went home, but Jesus went to the Mount of Olives to pray. Early in the morning, Jesus came to the temple again. As people of all ages gathered around, Jesus sat down and began to teach them as rabbis did.

The religious leaders strode up to where Jesus was teaching, dragging a frightened woman with them. They forced her to stand in front of the crowd so everyone could see her. One leader said to Jesus, "This woman has done wrong. The Law of Moses says we should kill her by stoning. What do you say?" The leaders were trying to see if Jesus would insist on keeping the law or not.

Jesus didn't answer. Instead he bent down and started writing on the ground with his finger. Jesus continued to write on the ground, saying nothing. But the leaders kept asking. Jesus straightened up and said, "Let the person who has not sinned be the first one to throw a stone at her." Then Jesus bent down again and continued writing on the ground.

When the people heard Jesus' words they each, one by one, put down their stones and walked away. Finally only the woman remained.

Jesus stood and looked at her. He said, "Where has everyone gone? Is anyone going to punish you?"

"No one, sir," the woman replied.

"I do not punish you either," Jesus said. "Go on your way and do what is right and good."

Wonder: What do you think Jesus was writing on the ground? I wonder how it felt to be forgiven by Jesus.

Explore

Find a stone to hold and think about who you wish would get punished. Then lay the stone on the ground as a sign of God's forgiveness.

Explore

Jewish leaders included wealthy, elite *Sadducees*, who controlled politics and the Jerusalem temple; *Pharisees*, who were often synagogue leaders and encouraged strict observance of the Law; and *scribes*, who copied the Hebrew scriptures.

American Sign Language for *love*

Connect
Look in a sign language book or online to learn the signs for *love*, *heart*, *soul*, *mind*, and *strength*. Memorize Mark 12:29–31 using the signs that you have learned.

Love your neighbor

Mark 12:28–34

One day in Jerusalem, a scribe listened to Jesus talking with some Sadducees. The scribe thought Jesus gave good answers to their questions, and he had a question of his own. He said to Jesus, "There are many laws and commandments in our scriptures. Which one is the most important?"

Jesus answered the scribe: "The first commandment is this: the Lord our God is one. Love the Lord your God with all your heart, and with all your soul, and with all your mind, and with all your strength. The second commandment is: love your neighbor as yourself. These are the most important commandments of all."

The scribe said, "You are right, Teacher. There is no other God. And the most important thing is to love God with your whole self and to love others the way you love yourself. This is much more important than all the offerings or sacrifices a person could ever make."

Jesus said to the scribe, "You are close to the kingdom of God."

Everyone around was silent. No one dared to ask Jesus any more questions.

Wonder: I wonder what it means to love God with your whole self.

Explore

The prophets in the Old Testament often told the people of Israel to change their ways so they could be better followers of God. If you were a prophet, what words would you say to these people at the temple?

Prophets are sometimes disliked for speaking the truth. Jeremiah was lowered into a muddy cistern.

Connect
Sometimes we give by sharing our money.
What are other ways that you can give?

The widow's offering

Mark 12:41–44

Jesus was teaching in the temple. When he finished, he sat down near the temple's offering box and watched the people coming by. Some very rich people came along, and they put a lot of money in the box.

Then along came a poor woman, a widow. She stopped at the offering box and put in two small copper coins. These were worth about a penny.

Jesus saw all of this. He called the disciples and said to them, "The rich people who came by gave a lot of money, but they had much more money left. This poor woman gave only two coins, but those coins were everything she had. I tell you truly, this poor woman has given more than all the rest."

Wonder: Why did the woman give everything she had?

Caring for those in need

Matthew 25:31–46

Connect
When were you a stranger in a new situation?
Who welcomed you?

The Son of man will come in glory and he will be like a king sitting on a throne. All the people of the world will come to hear him.

To some people he will say,
"You are blessed.
For I was hungry and you gave me food.
I was thirsty and you gave me something to drink.
I was a stranger and you welcomed me.
I was naked and you gave me clothing.
I was sick and you took care of me.
I was in prison and you visited me."

Those people will ask the king, "Lord, when did see you hungry or thirsty and give you food and water? When did we welcome you or give you clothing? When did we see you sick or in prison and visit you?"

The king will answer, "When you cared for those who needed you, you cared for me."

And then the king will say to the other people,
"You have treated me badly.
I was hungry and you didn't give me food.
I was thirsty and you didn't give me anything to drink.
I was a stranger and you did not welcome me.
I was naked and you didn't give me clothing.
I was sick and you didn't take care of me.
I was in prison and you didn't visit me. "

Those people will ask the king, "Lord, when did we see you hungry or thirsty or a stranger or naked or sick or in prison? When did we not take care of you?"

And the king will answer, "When you did not take care of others who needed you—that is when you did not take care of me."

Wonder: Imagine Jesus' followers listening to these words. I wonder what surprised them about this story.

Explore

It's hard to remember that helping others is like helping Jesus. Think about people that your family could care for as though they were Jesus.

Jesus washes the disciples' feet

John 13:1–20

Connect

In Bible times sandaled feet got dirty from walking. Servants washed the feet of all who arrived. What household jobs do you do to serve your family?

Jesus knew that soon he was going to die while he was in Jerusalem. Having loved the people in the world he was determined to love them to the very end.

One evening, he was eating supper with the disciples. During the meal, Jesus got up from the table and took off his outer robe. He tied a towel around his waist. He poured water into a basin. Then Jesus began to wash the feet of each disciple, drying them with the towel.

When Jesus came to Simon Peter, Peter exclaimed, "Lord, you will never wash my feet."

Jesus said, "If you want to remain my disciple, then I must wash your feet."

"Then Lord," said Peter, "don't wash just my feet; wash my hands as well! Wash my head, too!"

Jesus told him, "A person who has already bathed is clean, except for the feet."

After he had washed their feet, Jesus sat down again and said, "Do you understand what I have done? I am your Lord and Teacher, and I have washed your feet like a servant. I did this to show you how you should serve others."

He went on, "Servants are not greater than their masters. Messengers are not greater than the one who sends them. Do the things I have taught you here and you will be blessed. Whoever serves a person I send, serves me. Whoever serves me, serves the one who sent me."

Wonder: I wonder why Simon Peter did not want Jesus to wash his feet.

The vine and the branches

John 15:1–17

Connect
How can we be like the disciples and stay connected to Jesus?

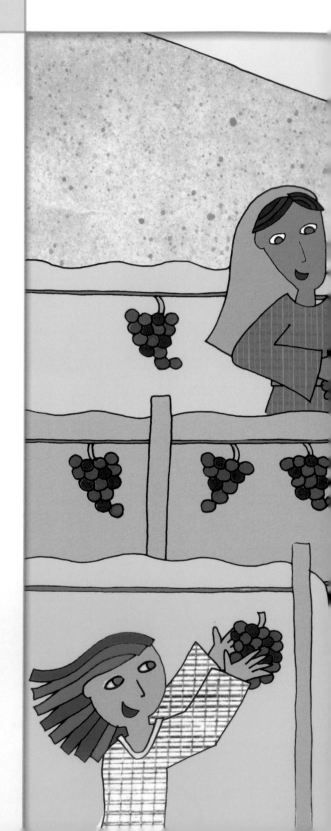

Grapevines are strong. They have roots in the soil. Branches grow out of each vine. The branches grow and grow with great green leaves. In a little while, the branches produce sweet grapes. But the branches need to stay attached to the vine. Without the vine, there are no green leaves. Without the vine, there is no fruit.

Jesus told his friends, "I am the vine. You are the branches. My Father is the vinegrower. I have shown you God's strong love. Stay close to my love.

"When vines have branches that don't bear fruit, the branches are removed. When branches do bear fruit, they are trimmed so they can produce even more fruit.

"I am the vine. You are the branches. You live in me and I live in you; we are connected. When you are connected to the vine, you will produce a lot of fruit. If you do not stay connected to the vine, you cannot produce any fruit. So stay connected to me.

"God loves me, and I have loved you. You can live in my love. The way to do this is to obey my commandments.

"Here is what I want you to do: love one another just as I have loved you. We show our greatest love when we can give up our lives for our friends. And you are my friends. I tell you this to make you joyful.

"I do not call you servants anymore. A servant doesn't know what the master is doing. But I have told you what I am doing; so now I call you my friends.

"You did not choose me; I chose you. And now I am sending you out to bear fruit in the world.

"Always remember the most important thing: love one another."

Wonder: How does the vine help the branches to grow fruit?

Explore

Jesus said God was like a vinegrower. What does a vinegrower do? Look up "growing grapes" to find out. Do you know of a sunny spot where you could grow grapes?

The Last Supper

Matthew 26:1–5, 14–30; Mark 14:1–2, 10–26; Luke 22:1–28

Connect
Look at the pictures of Jesus and the disciples. Imagine yourself in the scene. Where would you be sitting or standing? How would you feel?

It was getting close to the time of the Passover festival in Jerusalem. The temple leaders were looking for a way to put Jesus to death because of the way the people were flocking to him. They were happy when Jesus' disciple Judas came to them with an offer. In return for money, he would tell them when they could find Jesus with no crowds around.

Jesus sent Peter and John to arrange for the Passover festival. "Listen," said Jesus, "once you are in Jerusalem, you will meet a man carrying a jar of water. Follow him into the house that he enters. Say to the house's owner, 'The teacher needs a room to eat the Passover meal with his disciples.' He will show you a large room upstairs."

Peter and John went and found everything as Jesus had said. Together, they prepared the Passover meal.

That evening, Jesus and the disciples ate their Passover meal together. Jesus said, "I have been looking forward to this Passover, the last Passover before my great suffering." Then he held up the bread and thanked God. He broke off pieces for everyone. Then he said, "Take this bread and eat it. This is my body, which is given for you."

Then Jesus took a cup of wine. He thanked God for it and then shared it with the disciples. Jesus told them, "This is my blood, which will be poured out for many. When I die, there will be a new covenant between God and all people."

The disciples wondered why Jesus was talking about suffering. Then Jesus said, "One of you here is planning to betray me."

All the disciples except Judas were upset at hearing this. Each one asked him, "Surely, I am not the one, am I?"

Following the Passover tradition, when they finished the meal, they sang a hymn of praise together. Then they went out to the Mount of Olives.

Wonder: How was this meal different from other meals Jesus ate with his friends?

264

Explore

Jesus and the disciples celebrated Passover for the last time. How is this event, which we call the Last Supper, remembered in your church? Does it look similar to this meal, or is it quite different?

Explore

Many Christians walk "stations of the cross." This practice dates back as early as the fourth century. Stations feature paintings or sculptures to remind followers of Jesus' suffering and death.

Jesus' arrest

Matthew 26:36–75; Mark 14:32–72; Luke 22:39–65; John 18:1–27

Jesus and the disciples walked across the valley to the garden of Gethsemane where they often met. He told his disciples, "Sit here and stay awake while I go to pray. I feel very sad."

Jesus went a little distance away and he prayed to God for a way out of the terrible things to come. "But I will do what you want me to do," he said.

But the disciples could not stay awake. Three times Jesus asked them to stay awake. Three times they went to sleep instead of waiting for Jesus.

Judas came with a crowd of soldiers and temple police. They came with torches and carried swords and clubs. Jesus asked, "Who are you looking for?" The soldiers answered, "Jesus of Nazareth." Jesus replied, "I am Jesus." The soldiers immediately stepped back and fell to the ground.

Once more, Jesus asked who they were looking for. Again, the soldiers said they were looking for Jesus of Nazareth. "I told you that I am Jesus. So if you are looking for me, let my friends go free," said Jesus.

So in the dark of night, they bound Jesus and arrested him. First they took him to Annas, father–in–law of the high priest, and then to the home of Caiaphas, the high priest. Most of the disciples ran away but Peter followed from a distance.

Caiaphas held a sort of trial, where people told lies about Jesus. Jesus was silent until the high priest asked him, "Are you the Messiah, the Son of God?" Jesus answered, "I am." The temple leaders cried angrily, "He deserves to die."

Meanwhile, Peter sat outside the high priest's house. He was afraid and told everyone he did not know Jesus. When a rooster crowed, Peter remembered that earlier that evening Jesus had said to him: "Before the rooster crows, you will deny me three times." Peter wept bitterly.

Wonder: Imagine being with the disciples at Gethsemane, sleeping while Jesus prayed. I wonder why Jesus wanted his friends to stay awake while he prayed.

Explore

Ancient Jewish practices of mourning included fasting (not eating for a period of time), tearing clothing, and not bathing for several days. How do you mourn the loss of a loved one? Look up grieving practices in other cultures.

At left is the possible location of Golgotha, the place of the skull, where Jesus was crucified. Formations in the rocks can be seen to resemble a skull.

Connect

Have you experienced the death of a loved one? How can you remember that person in the way that you live today?

Jesus' death

Matthew 27; Mark 15; Luke 23; John 18:28–19:42

In the morning, the temple leaders took Jesus to Pilate, the Roman governor. After listening to Jesus, Pilate did not think that Jesus had done anything wrong. But the crowd shouted, "Crucify him! Crucify him!" So Pilate handed Jesus over to be killed. Pilate's soldiers beat Jesus and mocked him. Then the soldiers put Jesus on a cross between two bandits.

Jesus forgave those who were crucifying him, saying, "Father, forgive them for they do not know what they are doing."

As Jesus was dying he cried out, "Where are you, God? Are you there? Are you still with me?" Then Jesus died.

When Jesus breathed his last breath the sun went dark from noon to three. A Roman soldier stood there watching and hearing everything. He said, "Certainly this man was innocent."

Jesus' mother, Mary Magdalene, Salome, Mary the mother of James, and other friends watched the terrible things that happened to Jesus.

Later that day, Joseph of Arimathea took the body of Jesus down from the cross. Another follower named Nicodemus brought scented spices of myrrh and aloes. They wrapped Jesus' body in linen cloth and laid it in a tomb. It was Friday afternoon. Sabbath rest would begin at sundown. They rolled a stone in front of the tomb.

For Jesus' friends, all hope seemed gone.

Wonder: All Christians in the past and around the world remember the sad story of the crucifixion. I wonder why we tell this story. Look for signs that Jesus reached out in love despite this painful and shameful death.

Jesus is risen!

Matthew 28:1–10; Mark 16:1–8; Luke 24:1–12

Connect

Finish the sentence: "To me, Easter means . . ."

This same story is told a bit differently in each Gospel account. In the Gospel of Mark there is only one person in a white robe. In Mark, the women were so afraid they didn't tell anyone right away.

Mary Magdalene, Joanna, Mary the mother of James, and some other women got up while it was still dark. They carried their spices toward the tomb as the sun lit the eastern sky. The women were on their way to anoint the body of their dear friend Jesus. They had watched Joseph of Arimathea put Jesus' body into a tomb on Friday afternoon. Now it was the first day of the week, the day after the Sabbath.

They said to one another, "Who will roll away the stone for us from the entrance to the tomb?" But when they got to the tomb they found the stone rolled away. They did not find Jesus' body. Suddenly two men in dazzling clothes stood beside them.

The women were terrified and bowed their faces to the ground. The bright figures said, "Do not be afraid. You are looking for Jesus of Nazareth, who was crucified. He has been raised; he is not here! Do you remember? He told you while he was still in Galilee that on the third day he would rise again."

The women ran to tell Jesus' other friends.

The disciples didn't believe it. It seemed like a made-up story. Peter got up and ran to the tomb. The stone was rolled away. He stooped and looked inside the tomb. Sure enough, there were the linen cloths that Jesus' body had been wrapped in. But Jesus' body was not there. Peter went back home, amazed at what had happened.

Wonder: I wonder why the women were terrified. I wonder how long it took for them to feel joyful.

Explore

The women stayed close to Jesus and they were the first to spread the news that Jesus was alive. Read the story through twice, then try sharing the story with someone else.

Explore

God's love can bring life and peace even when things seem hopeless. With your family, make a scrapbook of stories and pictures where you can see love changing the world.

Connect
Music is an important part of Easter celebrations. Sing or listen to an Easter hymn.

Jesus appears to Mary Magdalene

John 20:1–18

The Gospel of John tells another story of Jesus' resurrection.

Early in the morning, while it was still dark, Mary Magdalene walked to the tomb.

When she got there, she saw that the stone had been rolled away from the opening. Mary hurried away and found Simon Peter and another of Jesus' disciples.

"They have taken our Lord from the tomb!" Mary told them. "I don't know where he is." The two disciples ran to the tomb. They looked inside and saw only the linen cloths lying there. The two disciples went back to their homes but Mary stayed by the tomb, weeping.

She bent over to look into the tomb. Two angels in white were sitting where Jesus' body had been. "Why are you crying?" they asked Mary.

"Someone has taken my Lord away and I don't know where he is." Just then, Mary turned and saw a man behind her. She didn't know that the man was Jesus.

He said to her, "Woman, why are you crying? Who are you looking for?"

Mary thought the man was the gardener. "Have you taken him away? Tell me where you put him and I will take him away."

Then Jesus said, "Mary!"

Mary turned and said, "Jesus! Teacher! It's you! You are alive!"

Jesus said, "Go to my brothers and say that I am going to my Father, to my God and your God."

Mary hurried to find the other disciples. "I have seen our Lord," she said. "Jesus is alive!"

Wonder: Why did Mary not recognize Jesus?

Walking on the Emmaus Road

Luke 24:13–35

Connect

Remember a time when you were upset or confused. How can talking with friends, family, or teachers help us?

Explore

The Emmaus Road story is often shown in Christian art. Look up "Emmaus Road images" and "road to Emmaus appearance" to see some examples. Below are works by Rembrandt van Rijn (top) and from the *St. Albans Psalter* by an unknown artist.

On the same day that some of the women had found an empty tomb, two of Jesus' friends were trudging along the road toward Emmaus. As they walked, they talked about everything that had happened in Jerusalem. Then, Jesus himself came along and joined them, but they didn't recognize him.

The stranger said, "What are you talking about?"

One of them, Cleopas, answered, "You must be the only person in Jerusalem who doesn't know what has been happening here."

The man said, "Tell me." And so they told him about how their teacher, Jesus of Nazareth, had suffered and died. "And," they said sadly, "we had hoped that he was the one who would save Israel."

"Another strange thing has happened," they added. "Some of the women went to the tomb this morning and found it empty. They said that angels had told them that Jesus was alive. Some of the other disciples went to the tomb. They also found it empty, but they did not see Jesus."

"You are foolish!" said the stranger. "Why won't you believe what the prophets have said about how the Messiah would suffer before entering into glory?"

Jesus talked with them about the words of the prophets the whole way to Emmaus. When they got to the village, the stranger walked on ahead of them. But Cleopas and the other disciple said, "Stay with us. The day is nearly over."

So he went in with them. At their meal, he took the bread, blessed it, and broke it. In that moment they recognized that it was Jesus—and then he vanished.

They said to each other, "Didn't you feel your heart burning inside you as he talked with us on the road? Our hearts knew it was Jesus even if our eyes did not recognize him."

The two disciples got up and ran the whole way back to Jerusalem. They told all the other disciples how they had met a stranger on the road and had recognized Jesus when he broke bread with them.

Wonder: Imagine how sad the friends were as they walked to Emmaus and how happy they were as they ran back to Jerusalem.

Explore

There is another story of a miraculous catch of fish in the Gospel of Luke. This one happened at the start of Jesus' ministry. Read Luke 5:1–11 for this great fishing story.

Jesus appears to disciples

John 21:1–14

Simon Peter and six other disciples were fishing in the Sea of Tiberias. They fished all night but didn't catch anything. Just after the sun came up, Jesus came to the water's edge and called out to them, "You haven't caught any fish, have you?"

"No," they answered. The disciples didn't know that it was Jesus talking to them!

"Throw your net to the other side of the boat and you will find some," Jesus told the tired fishermen.

The disciples did this. Now their net was so full of fish that they couldn't get it back into the boat!

Looking toward shore, one of the disciples cried out, "It is the Lord!" When Simon Peter heard this, he jumped into the water and headed for shore. The other disciples came in the boat, dragging the net full of fish. There were 153 large fish! And even with so many fish, the net was not torn.

When they came ashore, they saw that Jesus had built a fire. There was fish cooking on the fire, and bread to eat. Jesus said, "Come and have breakfast," and they shared the fish and bread.

Wonder: How would it feel to drag in such a huge catch of fish—especially after not catching anything all night long?

Jesus' ascension

Luke 24:50–53; Acts 1:1–11

Connect
The people had to wait for the gift of God's spirit. Pray: *God, give me patience when I have to wait for your spirit to lead me.*

After Jesus rose from the tomb, he showed himself to his disciples in Jerusalem. Sometimes Jesus' friends saw and talked with Jesus. Sometimes they didn't see him.

For forty days he came to his friends and taught them more about the kingdom of God. He said to them, "Stay here in Jerusalem until you receive a sign from God. Soon you will be baptized with the Holy Spirit."

The disciples asked, "Teacher, are you going to make Israel a kingdom again?"

Jesus answered, "This is not something you need to know. What is important is that soon the Holy Spirit will come to you and give you power. Then you will take my message to all of Judea and Samaria, and even to the very ends of the earth."

Then Jesus lifted up his hands and blessed his friends. As they were watching, he was lifted up into cloud and they could not see him any longer.

Suddenly, two men in white robes stood by them. They said, "Why do you stand looking up toward heaven? Jesus has been taken up into heaven. Someday he will return the same way."

The disciples went joyfully back to Jerusalem. They waited for the gift of God's spirit to come to them, and they went often to the temple to praise God.

Wonder: Why were Jesus' friends joyful after Jesus was lifted up?

Explore

Jesus' ascension happened forty days after the resurrection. Can you think of other places in the Bible where the number forty is mentioned? (Think of Noah, manna, Jesus in the wilderness.)

Pentecost

Acts 2:1–41

Connect

When have you experienced God's love? How can you be part of a group that welcomes others and shows God's love?

It was the day of Pentecost, or Shavuot. Faithful Jews from every nation came to Jerusalem. They were Parthians, Medes, Elamites. They came from Mesopotamia, Judea, Cappadocia, Pontus, Asia, Phrygia, Pamphylia, Egypt, and Libya. There were visitors from Rome, Crete, and Arabia. They came to Jerusalem from near and far to celebrate the time when God gave the law to Moses on Mount Sinai.

Jesus' friends gathered together, too. While they were in a room praying, they heard a sound like a rushing wind, and it filled the entire house where they were sitting. They looked around and saw what looked like little flames over each other's heads.

Then, God's gift of the Holy Spirit came to them. They were all filled with the Spirit and began to speak in other languages. The people from faraway lands heard these sounds and crowded around. They could all understand what the disciples were saying!

Many people were amazed and said, "How can this be? Aren't all these people from Galilee? How can they be speaking our languages? What does this mean?"

Some people just sneered. "These people are just drunk with wine," they said.

Peter stood up. "No, we are not drunk," he said. "God has given us the power of the Holy Spirit. Jesus was killed, but he has been raised up by God. He is the Messiah, God's chosen one."

The people were worried. They asked Peter and the others, "What should we do?"

Peter answered, "Turn away from your sins. Be baptized in the name of Jesus. You will be forgiven for the wrong things you have done and you will receive the gift of the Holy Spirit. This promise is for you, for your children, and for people who are far away. This promise is for everyone who is called by God."

That day, about three thousand people believed and were baptized.

Wonder: Imagine people from many nations gathering to worship.

Explore

Pentecost is the day that the Christian church celebrates God's gift of the Holy Spirit. What does your church do to celebrate Pentecost?

281

Connect

Think about the people that you often eat with. Is it your family? Your friends? Others? Who could you share food with?

282

Enough for all

Acts 2:42–47; 4:32–37

In the days after the coming of the Holy Spirit at Pentecost, people gathered about the apostles. The apostles preached about how Jesus, the Messiah, had risen from the dead. The people listened and were amazed because the apostles were doing many signs and wonders, the way Jesus had.

All those who believed shared all that they owned with each other. They would sell their possessions and give the money to others who needed it. They ate together in their homes gladly and generously.

Day after day, they worshiped together in the temple. Together, they praised God. And day by day, more people joined their community.

Everyone who owned lands or houses sold them and brought the money to the apostles to share with people who needed help. A man named Joseph sold a field, brought the money to the apostles, and laid it on the ground in front of them for them.

The people in the community gave joyfully to each other. What one person had owned now belonged to everyone. Now everyone had a place to live, and clothes to wear, and enough food to eat. They were filled with the Spirit of God.

Wonder: Why did more and more people want to join the community?

Peter, John, and a lame man

Acts 3:1–10

Explore
Like the man begging at the temple, many people today have barely enough to live. Read *Cups Held Out*, *Beatrice's Goat*, or another book about poverty.

Peter and John went to the temple to pray. They came across a man sitting next to the temple gate. Every day, his friends carried him to the gate because he could not walk. Every day, he called out, asking for money.

That day the man called to Peter and John, asking for money. Peter and John looked at the man, and Peter said to him, "Look at us."

The man looked up. He thought Peter and John would give him some money. But Peter told him, "I don't have any money. I have something even better to give you. In the name of Jesus, stand up and walk!"

Peter took the man by the hand. Just like that, the man's feet and ankles were strong. He stood up and walked! He entered the temple with Peter and John, walking and leaping and praising God.

The people inside the temple saw the man. They knew he was the man who used to sit at the gate and beg. They were amazed at what had happened. The man who had been lame had been healed. He could walk!

Wonder: Imagine what it was like for the man to walk and jump.

284

Connect
Praise God for the wonderful things in your life.
Walk, jump, leap, and praise!

Connect

When have you heard someone tell a lie about another person?
Think about a time when you wanted to get someone in trouble.
What makes people mistreat others?

Explore
Look up Luke 23:34. Compare this with Stephen's prayer.

Stephen's story

Acts 6–7

The community of Jesus continued to grow. Some people began to complain. They said, "Our widows are not being taken care of. They are not getting their fair share of food."

The twelve apostles called everyone together. They said, "We need to keep praying and teaching, but we must also make sure that everyone is treated fairly. Friends, you must choose seven people who are wise and full of God's spirit. They will be in charge of serving the food fairly."

The people were happy with this idea. They chose Stephen and six others to work together.

Stephen was full of God's spirit and he did great wonders and signs. But some people did not like him and wanted to get rid of him. They began to tell lies about him.

Stephen was brought before the Jewish court, the Sanhedrin. When the court looked at Stephen, they saw that his face was like the face of an angel. But still, the high priest asked Stephen if he had lied.

Stephen answered, "Friends, listen to me! Let me tell you a story. Our ancestor Abraham followed God. But the grandsons of his son sold their brother Joseph into slavery. God saved Joseph and made him a ruler of Egypt. When there was no food in other lands, Joseph brought his family to live in Egypt.

"Years passed, and there were more and more Israelites in Egypt. Then a new, cruel ruler made them all slaves. But God called Moses to lead them out of Egypt to freedom. The people should have been grateful. But they complained and stopped worshiping God."

Stephen continued, "You people here, you have also disobeyed God. You betrayed Jesus and killed him."

When Stephen said this, the members of the court were furious. They dragged Stephen out of the city and threw stones at him. Stephen prayed, "Lord, forgive these people." Then, after asking Jesus to receive his spirit, Stephen died.

Wonder: The illustration shows a joyful time at the beginning of the story. How did the story change? Why did people become so upset about what Stephen said and did?

Philip and the Ethiopian official

Acts 8:4–8, 26–40

Connect

How can you share the story of Jesus? What is the good news that you would like to share?

The followers of Jesus went from place to place telling people about Jesus. Philip preached and healed many people. Many people listened to him and believed what he said about Jesus.

Then an angel said to Philip, "Go to the road that runs between Jerusalem and the city of Gaza." Philip did what the angel said. As he waited by the road, along came a chariot.

Inside the chariot was an official from the court of the queen of Ethiopia! He had gone to Jerusalem to worship and was now returning home. He was sitting in his chariot and reading a scroll from the prophet Isaiah.

The Spirit said to Philip, "Go; get into that chariot." So Philip ran up to the chariot. He asked, "Do you understand this scroll that you are reading?"

The Ethiopian official answered, "How can I understand it unless someone explains it to me?" He invited Philip into his chariot. The scripture he was reading went like this: "Like a sheep, he was led to the butcher. Silent, he did not open his mouth. He was humiliated and denied justice. Even his life was taken away."

The official asked, "Who is the prophet writing about?"

Philip explained the words of the prophet and told the man about Jesus.

As they rode along, they came to some water. The official said, "Look, here's some water! Why can't I be baptized right now?" He commanded the chariot to stop. The two of them went into the water, and Philip baptized him right then and there.

After this, God's spirit took Philip away. The Ethiopian official continued on his way home. He was very happy.

Wonder: Imagine being so excited about getting baptized and learning about Jesus.

A portion of the Isaiah scroll discovered in a cave near the Dead Sea

Explore

The Ethiopian official was a very important official. He was wealthy enough to have an Isaiah scroll, which he carried with him on this trip. Look on a map to see where Ethiopia is located. He would have come a long way to Jerusalem!

Explore

Damascus was the capital of Syria. Saul's journey from Jerusalem to Damascus may have taken about six days. Learn about modern-day Damascus. Straight Street is mentioned in the book of Acts. Is there still a street by this name?

Connect

When Saul chose to follow Jesus, he joined the very people he had hated. When have you seen someone make a big change in how they act?

Saul sees the light

Acts 9:1–31

Saul really did not like followers of Jesus. He asked the high priest to let him arrest believers in Damascus and bring them back to Jerusalem in chains.

Saul was going to Damascus when suddenly a light flashed. He fell to the ground and heard a voice saying, "Saul, why do you persecute me?"

"Who are you, Lord?" Saul asked.

"I am Jesus. You are persecuting me. Get up and enter the city. You will be told what to do."

Saul got up, but he could not see. People traveling with him led him by the hand to Damascus. There Saul did not eat or drink for three days—and he still could not see.

Then God told Ananias, a disciple in Damascus, to go to Saul. Ananias protested, "This man has done evil things!" He knew Saul could put him in prison.

But the Lord said, "Go! I have chosen Saul."

So Ananias went. He helped Saul and said, "Brother Saul, the Lord Jesus, who appeared to you on the road, has sent me so that you can see again and be filled with the Holy Spirit."

Immediately Saul could see. He was baptized, ate some food, and felt strong again.

Saul went to the synagogue in Damascus and told everyone about Jesus. This amazed people. They said, "Isn't this the man who has been persecuting the followers of Jesus?"

Some people did not like Saul's message about Jesus and wanted to kill him. But Saul learned of their plot. The disciples helped him escape from the city by lowering him in a basket from the wall.

Back in Jerusalem, Saul wanted to meet believers, but they were afraid of him. They thought he pretended to follow Jesus so he could arrest them.

But Barnabas believed Saul and brought him to the apostles. He told about what had happened to Saul. Saul continued to speak about Jesus. Once again, people wanted to kill him. And once again his new brothers and sisters helped him escape.

Wonder: I wonder why Saul persecuted Christians. Imagine being Ananias. Would you have wanted to help Saul?

Explore

Find out about clinics in your community that offer medical services to people who don't have regular doctors.

Great Sea

GALILEE

Joppa

Jerusalem

JUDEA

Connect

Who are some people in your community or church who do acts of kindness like Tabitha did? Consider doing one "random act of kindness" today and try not to let anyone know who did it.

Tabitha

Acts 9:32–43

Peter was busy. He traveled here and there, visiting the followers of Jesus in many towns.

In the town of Lydda there was a man named Aeneas. For eight years, Aeneas had been paralyzed and could not get out of his bed. Peter said to Aeneas, "Aeneas, Jesus Christ heals you. Get up and make your bed!" Many people believed in Jesus when they saw Aeneas healed and walking.

In the nearby town of Joppa lived a follower of Jesus, a disciple named Tabitha, or Dorcas, who spent her life doing good work and kind acts to help others. Sadly, she became very sick and died. Her friends were mourning. When they heard that Peter was nearby, they sent two messengers to ask him, "Please come to us quickly." Peter went to Joppa with the messengers.

When he got there, they took him upstairs. Several women were there, weeping for Tabitha. They showed Peter the clothing Tabitha had made. Peter sent them all outside, then knelt down and prayed. He turned to Tabitha's body and said, "Tabitha, get up." She opened her eyes and sat up! Peter held out his hand and helped her out of bed. Then he called the others to show them she was alive.

Everyone in Joppa heard the story and many people became followers of Jesus. Meanwhile, Peter stayed in Joppa for some time with Simon, a tanner.

Wonder: I wonder what Tabitha's friends expected Peter would do when they sent for him.

What are characteristics of people whose lives have been touched by the Holy Spirit? Look up the list of the "fruit of the Holy Spirit" mentioned in Galatians 5:22–23.

A monument to a Roman centurion. Centurions were Roman officers in charge of a company of soldiers.

Connect
Who do you think your community might consider unclean or unacceptable?

Cornelius and Peter

Acts 10

A man named Cornelius, a member of the Roman army, lived in Caesarea. He was a Gentile, but he believed in God. He prayed to God and helped people who were poor.

One afternoon, an angel appeared to him and said, "Your prayers have been heard. Send men to Joppa to bring back a man named Peter." So Cornelius called his men. He explained the angel's message and sent them to Joppa.

Peter, who was a Jew, was teaching other Jews in Joppa about God. Usually, Peter's people and Cornelius's people did not meet or speak to each other.

Now Simon Peter also had a vision. He saw all kinds of animals being lowered from heaven in a large sheet, even animals Jews weren't allowed to eat. A voice from heaven said, "Get up, Peter, and eat." This happened three times.

Meanwhile, Cornelius's men arrived at the gate asking for Peter. God's spirit said to Peter, "Look, three men are searching for you. Go with them and do not worry, because I have sent them."

Peter agreed to go with them to meet Cornelius, who had called his family and friends together in expectation. When Peter and the servants arrived, Cornelius went out to welcome Peter and fell on the ground to worship him. Peter said, "Stand up; I am only a man."

Cornelius told him, "The angel said I should send for you. Now, all of us are here to listen to what God has sent you to say."

Peter said, "Now I know that God wants everyone to hear about Jesus. It does not matter who they are or where they live. The good news about Jesus is for anyone who wants to follow God."

As Peter spoke, the Holy Spirit came upon the group. The Jews were amazed that the Holy Spirit came to the Gentiles as well. Peter asked, "Can anyone withhold the water for baptizing people who have received the Holy Spirit?" So Cornelius and his family were baptized in the name of Jesus Christ.

Wonder: I wonder how Peter and Cornelius felt after they met and became friends.

A rescue from prison

Acts 12:1–17

Connect

If you were in prison for something you believed God told you to do, and were freed like Peter, whose house would you go to first?

King Herod attacked the believers. He had James killed with a sword. When he saw that this pleased the people, he arrested Peter, too. He put Peter in prison, planning to kill him. The church prayed fervently to God for Peter.

The night before Herod was going to have Peter put to death, Peter slept bound with two chains, between two soldiers, and with more guards at the door.

Suddenly an angel of the Lord appeared, and a light shone in Peter's prison cell. The angel tapped Peter on the side and woke him, saying, "Get up quickly." The chains fell off! The angel told him to put on his sandals and cloak. Peter followed the angel, but he thought it was a vision or dream. They passed the first guard . . . they passed the second guard . . . then the iron gate leading into the city opened all by itself.

They left the prison and walked along a lane, when suddenly the angel left. Peter realized this was really happening! God had rescued him from Herod!

Peter went to the house of Mary, where many believers were gathered to pray. He knocked on the door and a maid named Rhoda answered. She was so happy and overwhelmed to hear Peter's voice that, instead of opening the gate, she ran in and announced that Peter was there.

Everyone thought she must be crazy! She kept insisting, so they said, "It's his angel." After all, Peter was in jail! Meanwhile, Peter kept knocking.

Finally they opened the gate. Everyone was amazed! Peter told them how the Lord had rescued him. Then he left and went to another place.

Wonder: Who do you think was most amazed: Peter, Rhoda, or the believers at Mary's house?

Explore

King Herod put Peter in jail for preaching about Jesus. In what countries today might people be put in jail for preaching about Jesus? Explore "persecution of Christians" online to find recent examples of countries where Christians face persecution.

Explore

Follow Paul's first missionary journey on a map. What present-day countries are in that part of the world?

Paul and Barnabas travelled in a ship similar to this one.

Paul's first missionary journey

Acts 13–14

As Saul traveled and talked about Jesus, he took a new name. He used his Greek name, Paul. While he was in Syria, in the city of Antioch, the followers of Jesus sang and prayed, and God's spirit told them, "Send Barnabas and Paul to tell others the good news about Jesus and God's love."

The people of the church gathered around Paul and Barnabas. They laid their hands on them and prayed for them. Then Paul and Barnabas sailed away on their long journey. On the island of Cyprus, they traveled from synagogue to synagogue, telling people about Jesus.

From Cyprus, they sailed to Perga and then to another city called Antioch, in Pisidia. They told the people there the good news about Jesus. They said, "God was with our people in Egypt and as they traveled in the wilderness. God was with our people in Canaan, giving them judges and kings to rule them. And God is with us now. We have good news. Jesus came to show God's love."

The next week, the whole city gathered to hear Paul and Barnabas. Some people became followers of Jesus. But others became angry. Paul and Barnabas had to leave Antioch.

They traveled on to Iconium. They preached in the synagogue, telling people about Jesus. They did amazing things to show people their words were true, and many of the people became followers of Jesus. But others became angry and wanted to hurt them. So Paul and Barnabas escaped to Lystra.

In Lystra, Paul healed a man who could not walk. Many people believed the good news he shared. Others were angry and tried to kill him. But the followers of Jesus protected Paul.

Next, he went with Barnabas to Derbe. They spoke to the believers there and helped them grow stronger in their faith.

Then they sailed back home to Antioch. The believers there gathered to hear about the journey. Paul and Barnabas told them all about what God had done and about the many people on their travels who had become followers of Jesus.

Wonder: How could Paul and Barnabas be bold and joyful when they were treated badly by others?

Explore

This story mentions that Lydia went to the river to pray. Can you think of other stories where people went somewhere special to pray? Where did Jesus pray? Where do you pray?

Connect

Paul and Silas showed kindness while they were in jail. What are some unusual places where you could show kindness?

Mission in Philippi

Acts 16:11–40

On another journey, Paul traveled with a believer named Silas. The two of them sailed to Philippi and stayed there for a while, praying and telling people about Jesus.

One Sabbath, they went to the river to pray. They sat down and spoke to the women who were gathered there. One woman named Lydia was listening. She was from a city called Thyatira and she had a business selling purple cloth.

Lydia was a follower of God, and she listened eagerly as Paul and Silas talked about Jesus. Then she and all the people in her house were baptized.

Lydia had a house large enough for guests. She said to Paul and Silas, "Come stay at my house."

Another day, when Paul and Silas were going to a place to pray, Paul healed a slave girl. Her owners were angry that Paul had interfered with their slave. They dragged Paul and Silas to the city rulers in the marketplace. They said, "These men are disturbing our city. They are telling people to do things that are not legal here."

The city rulers had Paul and Silas beaten and thrown into jail. They told the jailer, "Make sure they do not get out."

Paul and Silas sang and prayed while they were in jail. The other prisoners listened. Suddenly, at midnight, the earth shook and the jail doors opened.

The jailer woke up and was afraid that his prisoners had escaped. But Paul and Silas had not run away. Instead, Paul shouted, "We are all here." Then Paul and Silas began to tell the jailer about Jesus.

The jailer took Paul and Silas home with him and took care of them. Then, the jailer and his family were baptized.

In the morning, the city rulers apologized to Paul and Silas and let them go. Paul and Silas went back to Lydia's house. After they had seen and talked with their friends there, they left and continued their travels.

Wonder: Imagine singing praises to God while in chains.

301

The church in Corinth

Acts 18:1–17; 1 Corinthians 13

Connect
How do you show love to yourself, others, God, and creation?

Corinth was another city that Paul visited. There were many believers in that large city. And there were many other people who wanted to learn more about Jesus.

Every Sabbath, Paul told people about Jesus. He found that Gentiles, people who were not Jews, were interested in what he had to say. So he began to spend more time teaching them. Many Jews also listened to Paul. He met Titius Justus, who lived next door to the synagogue, and Crispus and Sosthenes, who were synagogue officials. Crispus and everyone in his house were baptized.

One night, Paul had a dream. In the dream God said, "Do not be afraid. I am with you. Speak and do not be silent. Many people in this city will follow Jesus."

Paul stayed in Corinth for a year and a half. The church there grew strong as Paul continued to teach about God.

When Paul left Corinth, he did not forget the church there. He wrote his friends a letter.

Paul's friends in Corinth read the letter out loud.

To Sosthenes and to the church in Corinth:
We can do lots of great things, but love is more important than doing something great. If we don't have love, we have nothing.

Love is patient; love is kind; love is not jealous or boastful or arrogant or rude.

Love does not insist on getting its own way; it does not get annoyed or angry. Love is never glad about wrongdoing; love is happy when people act honestly.

Love never ends.

Have faith, hope, and love. But the greatest of these is love.

The grace of the Lord Jesus be with you. My love be with all of you in Christ Jesus,

Paul

Wonder: What letter do you think the people of Corinth wrote back to Paul?

302

The remains of the synagogue at Sardis

Explore

Sabbath is a day of rest and worship for Jews. A synagogue is a place to worship and learn about God. Find out about synagogues today. Is there one near you?

Aquila and Priscilla

Acts 18:1–3, 18–28

Connect

We each have gifts that can be used for God's work. One gift that Aquila and Priscilla shared was the gift of hospitality. What gift can you share?

Aquila and Priscilla were husband and wife. They were tentmakers, and they lived and worked in Rome, Italy. But then the emperor Claudius ordered all Jews to leave Rome. So Priscilla and Aquila came to Greece and settled in Corinth.

When Paul came to Corinth, he met Aquila and Priscilla. Paul was also a tentmaker, and so they invited him to stay at their home. Paul stayed for a long time, making tents with Aquila and Priscilla and teaching about Jesus to people all over the city.

After a year and a half, Paul left to teach about Jesus in other cities. And Priscilla and Aquila left with him! When the ship docked at Ephesus, the three of them got off. Paul talked to the Jews in the synagogue, and then went on his way.

Aquila and Priscilla stayed in Ephesus. They spoke to many believers in Ephesus. One day they met a man named Apollos, who was a very enthusiastic follower of Jesus.

Apollos knew all about scripture and spoke very well. He wanted to tell everyone about Jesus even though he didn't quite understand everything. When he began to talk in the synagogue, Priscilla and Aquila took him aside. They explained things about Jesus that Apollos had not understood before.

Because of Paul, Priscilla and Aquila were better able to tell people about Jesus. And because of Priscilla and Aquila, Apollos was better able to tell people about Jesus. The followers of Jesus helped each other, and together they built up the church of Jesus in the world.

Wonder: Imagine people meeting each other and discovering other followers of Jesus.

The temple of Apollo in Corinth

Explore

Aquilla and Priscilla are mentioned in other places. Look up these Bible passages and learn the names of other early Christians: 2 Timothy 4:19–22; Romans 16:1–5; 1 Corinthians 16:13–20.

Setting sail

Acts 27–28

Connect

Think about a hard time that you experienced. Pray: *God, thank you that you are always with me, through the good times and bad times.*

Paul was going to Italy by ship, but he was not free to go on his own. He was being taken as a prisoner to be tried in the court of the emperor. The centurion in charge of the soldiers on the ship was named Julius. Julius grew to like Paul and treated him kindly.

The ship moved slowly because the winds were against it. Winter was coming and sailing became riskier. When the ship landed at Fair Havens on the island of Crete, Paul told them that they should stop there. He said, "This voyage will be dangerous and we will suffer heavy losses."

But the pilot and the ship owner wanted to find a safer place to spend the winter. So they sailed on—but soon a violent wind caught the ship. The crew threw cargo overboard. They threw the ship's tackle overboard. The storm lasted for days and the people on the ship lost all hope.

"Keep up your courage," said Paul. "Last night an angel told me that God is with us. We will lose the ship but all the people will be safe."

Finally after fourteen days of stormy weather, they neared land. Paul said, "Everyone should eat. It will help you survive." He gave thanks to God, broke bread, and began to eat. All the people on board, 276 of them, felt more hopeful and ate.

In the morning the ship struck a reef, but everyone grabbed pieces of wood and made it safely to the island of Malta. The island people built a fire so the travelers could get warm. They gave them food to eat and places to sleep. Paul told the people of Malta about Jesus and prayed for them too. Many people came to Paul to be healed.

Three months later Paul and the others set sail for Italy in a new ship. In Rome, Paul lived for two years under house arrest with a soldier nearby all the time. He welcomed everyone who came to his house. He boldly told them all about Jesus Christ and the kingdom of God.

Wonder: Think about all the things Paul faced: being arrested, violent storms, being shipwrecked, living under guard in a new city. How did he know that God was with him?

Malta is home to megalithic temples constructed thousands of years before Paul was shripwrecked there.

Explore
With others, pray an *examen* prayer. People have prayed this type of prayer for centuries. It is a good prayer for the end of each day. Tell God the things that made you "glad, sad, and sorry" today.

Galatia is in modern Turkey. Apricots, cherries, mandarin oranges, dates, blackberries, and quince are among the fruits grown there. Eat some of these fruits as you think about fruits of the Spirit.

Growing the fruit of the Spirit

Galatians 5:13–26

Paul wrote to the people in Galatia:

My brothers and sisters, God wants you to be free! But do not use your freedom only for yourself. You must serve each other lovingly. There is one commandment that sums up all the rules of our faith: Love your neighbor as yourself.

Those who follow Jesus Christ think of others instead of just thinking about themselves.

Feed your spirit, not just your body.

Treat each other with respect.

Worship God, not idols.

Instead of thinking you are better than others, show kindness.

Instead of showing jealousy, show love.

Instead of arguing, listen to each other.

Showing God's spirit is like being a tree that bears good fruit. The fruit of the Spirit is love, joy, peace, patience, kindness, generosity, faithfulness, gentleness, and self-control.

Let us all let the Spirit grow in us and bear fruit. When we live this way, we show that we belong to Jesus Christ.

Wonder: Imagine the goodness of ripe fruit on trees. Now picture people being loving, joyful, patient, and kind.

Explore

Look for the stories of Noah, Abraham and Sarah, Moses, Rahab, David, and Samuel in this book. Count how many stories there are about Jesus!

Connect

What people of faith are your heroes? What is it about them that you appreciate?

Cloud of witnesses

Hebrews 11:1–12:2

Faith is being able to believe in something that you cannot see with your eyes. Faith helps us understand that God made the world. There are many people of faith whose stories are told in the Bible.

Noah was a person of faith. He believed God's warning and built an ark.

Abraham and Sarah were people of faith. They obeyed God and journeyed to a new land, even though they did not know where they were headed.

Moses was a person of faith. He listened when God called him to help the Israelite people. Moses led the people out of Egypt to the land God had prepared for them.

Rahab was a woman of faith. She believed in God and sheltered some of the people of God in her home.

Many other people of faith are named in the scriptures, like David and Samuel and the prophets. And there have been many others, whose names we do not know, who also had faith and followed God, even when others made fun of them or persecuted them.

There are also many stories about Jesus. Jesus was the pioneer of our faith. He did not give up when he knew he would die on the cross. Jesus knew that he would later have great joy. He is now with God.

We are surrounded by a great cloud of people who have followed God. They have all run the race of faith. Let's get rid of anything that would weigh us down, so that we also can run the race of faith. As we run, Jesus is always ahead of us, Jesus who shows us how to be people of faith.

Wonder: I wonder what it means for Jesus to be the pioneer of our faith.

Respecting others

James 2:1–13

Connect
How can you show kindness and love to everyone, no matter if they are rich or poor?

The book of James in the Bible was a letter written to help church people know how to live. It says:

If two new people come to your church, do you treat them the same? What if one is dressed in fancy clothes and wears gold jewelry and the other person has clothes that are old and dirty?

What if you said to the well-dressed person, "Please sit here in this comfortable seat, my friend!" And what if you ignored the poor person in dirty clothes or said, "You can sit here on the floor." If you did that, you would be judging that the rich person is worth more than the poor person. But God has no favorites. God loves everyone.

Listen, my brothers and sisters. Pay attention. God has given a lot of faith to those who are poor and looked down upon.

To follow God's ways, you must treat everyone the way you would like to be treated. You do really well if you obey the royal law, the scripture that says, "Love others as you love yourself."

If you judge others, you will be judged.

If you want to be treated kindly, treat others kindly.

Kindness is better than judgment.

Remember the royal law, and treat everyone with love and fairness, just as you want to be treated.

Wonder: Why would God give a lot of faith to those who are poor?

Explore

Find out more about your community. Who are the people who are poor or looked down upon? What could your family do to treat them well?

Explore

John's vision also included a city that had walls of jasper, gates of pearl, and golden streets. God's light filled the city. Find a song or hymn based on a passage from Revelation.

314

Connect

Draw a picture of your dreams for a new heaven and a new earth.

New heaven and new earth

Revelation 1:1–2; 21:1–7; 22:8–9

A man named John was sent to the island of Patmos, away from family and friends, as punishment for following Jesus. While he was there he had a vision. This is what he saw and heard:

There was a new heaven and a new earth. I saw God's holy city of Jerusalem coming down out of heaven. It looked as festive as a bride at her wedding.

I heard a loud voice saying, "This is God's home. God will live here with the people and wipe everyone's tears away.

"There will be no more dying. There will be no more crying. There will be no more pain. All those things will be gone.

"See, I am making all things new!

"I am the beginning and the end.

"I will give the water of life to those who are thirsty.

"I will be their God, and they will be my children."

John heard and saw these and many other strange things in his vision. He fell down to worship at the feet of the angel who showed them to him. But the angel said, "Don't worship me. Worship God!"

Wonder: Look carefully at the illustration. What details of John's vision can you see in this picture?

Suficiente comida junto al mar

Marcos 6.30–44

Conectarse

Cuando compartimos, suceden cosas maravillosas. ¿Ha participado alguna vez en la recaudación de fondos para combatir el hambre en el mundo? Oración: *Dios, ayúdanos a preocuparnos por los demás, para que los recursos alcancen para todos.*

Los discípulos de Jesús emprendieron un viaje para enseñar. Luego regresaron a contarle a Jesús cómo les había ido. Estaban tan ocupados, con tanta gente que iba y venía, que no tenían tiempo siquiera para comer. Jesús les dijo: —Vengan conmigo a un lugar tranquilo donde puedan descansar un rato. De modo que fueron en una barca a un lugar donde podrían estar a solas.

Pero muchos los reconocieron y sabían hacia dónde iban. Fueron de prisa a ese lugar a pie, mientras que Jesús y sus discípulos fueron en barca. Cuando Jesús y sus discípulos llegaron a la otra orilla, una multitud de gente ya estaba allí.

Jesús sintió compasión por toda esa gente, porque vio que eran como ovejas sin pastor. En vez de despedirlos, comenzó a enseñarles.

Luego se empezó a hacer tarde y los discípulos se le acercaron a Jesús.—Despide a las personas, que vayan a los pueblos cercanos —dijeron—. Así podrán comprarse algo de comer.

Jesús respondió: — Denles ustedes mismos algo de comer.

Los discípulos se alarmaron. —¿Cómo podremos comprar comida para toda esta gente? — preguntaron.

Jesús dijo: —Vayan y vean cuánto pan tienen. Los discípulos encontraron cinco panes y dos pescados.

Entonces Jesús les mandó a los discípulos que hicieran que la gente se sentara en grupos sobre la hierba verde. Las personas, cinco mil en total, se sentaron en grupos de cien y de cincuenta.

Jesús tomó los pescados y los panes, miró hacia el cielo y bendijo la comida. Partió los panes en trozos y se los dio a los discípulos. También repartió el pescado.

Los discípulos repartieron la comida a todos los grupos de personas. Todos comieron hasta quedar satisfechos. Después los discípulos recogieron las sobras y, asombrosamente, juntaron doce canastas llenas de pan y pescado.

Yo me pregunto... Me pregunto por qué la gente tenía tantas ganas de estar con Jesús.

Explorar

Esta historia se cuenta también en Mateo 14.13-21, Lucas 9.12-17 y Juan 6.4-13, pero las versiones no son todas iguales. Encuentre la versión en la que un niño comparte su comida con la multitud.

Panes y Peces mosaico de Tabgah, Israel

317

Story picture illustrators

Additional illustrations and photos

87. Mary Lou Cramer.

90. Rebecca Thornburgh.

93. Kimberly Bowles.

94. Kimberly Bowles.

97. Martin Poole/Photodisc/Thinkstock.

100. Sergiy Zavgorodny/iStoockphoto/Thinkstock.

102. Kimberly Bowles.

104. Benny Gool.

106. Larry Nolt.

108. LiquidLibrary/Thinkstock.

111. Ingrid Hess.

113. Len Epstein.

114. Eldad Carin/iStockphoto/Thinkstock.

117. Katarzyna krzysztof Dedek/Hemera/Thinkstock.

127. Hemera Technologies/Thinkstock.

130. Fuse/Thinkstock.

133. mujun/iStockphoto/Thinkstock.

135. Sherry Neidigh.

139. Orchi/Wikimedia Commons.

143. matthewennisphotography/iStockphoto/Thinkstock.

145. SZE FEI WONG/iStockphoto/Thinkstock.

149. Jan Luyken, *Martyrs Mirror*, p. 873, Herald Press.

150. Fuse/Thinkstock.

156. Ho Ho Kee/iStockphoto/Thinkstock.

159. Eric Michaud/iStockphoto/Thinkstock.

160. Gwen Stamm.

165. Kai Chiang/iStockphoto/Thinkstock.

166. Joy Dunn Keenan.

168. Joy Dunn Keenan.

169. Vadim Kozlovsky/Hemera/Thinkstock.

175. Vladimir Khirman/iStockphoto/Thinkstock.

176. Digital Vision/Thinkstock.

179. Allan Eitzen.

180. DesignPics.

182. Rebecca Thornburgh.

185. Berthold Werner/Wikimedia Commons.

186. Israel Antiquities Authority, permission requested.

188. Mindy Chung Wai Meng/iStockphoto/Thinkstock.

195. Catherine Yeulet/iStockphoto/Thinkstock.

197. Rebecca Thornburgh.

200. Len Epstein.

202. JuanmoninoiStockphoto/Thinkstock.

205. Monkey Business Images Ltd/Valueline/Thinkstock.

206. Kimberly Bowles.

209. Ingrid Hess.

211. Left: Len Epstein; right: Merrill Miller.

213. Surachet Meewaew/iStockphoto/Thinkstock.

214. Joel Carillet/iStockphoto/Thinkstock.

216. Comstock/Thinkstock.

218. Gabhor Utomo.

220. Len Epstein.

222. Left: Allan Eitzen; right: Jacob Wackerhausen/ iStockphoto/Thinkstock.

225. Einsamer Schütze/Wikimedia Commons.

227. Petro Feketa/iStockphoto/Thinkstock.

228. Stockbyte/Thinkstock.

230. Hallgerd/iStockphoto/Thinkstock.

232. Left: Wavebreakmedia Ltd/Thinkstock; right: Len Epstein.

234. Len Epstein.

237. Ed Wallace.

238. Len Epstein.

241. Len Epstein.

245. Eitan f, Wikimedia Commons.

246. monkeybusinessimages/iStockphoto/Thinkstock.

248. Nancy Munger.

253. Benjamin O'Neal/iStockphoto/Thinkstock.

256. Harriet Miller.

259. Len Epstein.

261. Dmitriy Shironosov/Hemera/Thinkstock.

263. Sherry Neidigh.

265. Keith Neely.

266. Kate Cosgrove.

268. Footballkickit at en.wikipedia.

271. Rebecca Thornburgh.

272. Len Epstein.

276. Kate Cosgrove.

279. Gwen Stamm.

281. Len Epstein.

282. Comstock Images/Thinkstock.

285. Morgan Lane Studios/iStockphotos/Thinkstock.

286. BananaStock/Thinkstock.

289. Wikimedia Commons.

292. Steve Hix/Fuse/Thinkstock.

294. Wikimedia Commons.

297. Harriet Miller.

298. John Pittaway.

300. Nancy Munger.

303. Wikimedia Commons.

305. Wikimedia Commons.

307. Berthold Werner/Wikimedia Commons.

308. Thinkstock.

310. Allan Eitzen.

313. Gabhor Utomo.

314. Kate Cosgrove.

317. Left: Len Epstein; right: Merrill Miller.

320. Suzanne Harden.